God Man Messiah
"It Is Finished"

DAN COFLIN

God Man Messiah:
It Is Finished
Copyright © 2020
Published by Coflin Family Publishing
ISBN: 978-0-9970643-1-5
Scripture quotations from the following sources:
Unless otherwise indicated, all Scripture quotations are taken from the *King James Version* of the Bible.
"Scripture quotations taken from the Amplified® Bible, Copyright © 1954, 1958, 1962, 1964, 1965, 1987 by The Lockman Foundation Used by permission." (www.Lockman.org)
All scripture quotations in the publication are from the Contemporary English Version Copyright © 1991, 1992, 1995 by American Bible Society, Used by Permission.
"Scripture quotations taken from the New American Standard Bible®, Copyright © 1960, 1962, 1963, 1968, 1971, 1972, 1973, 1975, 1977, 1995 by The Lockman Foundation Used by permission." (www.Lockman.org)
THE HOLY BIBLE, NEW INTERNATIONAL VERSION®, NIV® Copyright © 1973, 1978, 1984, 2011 by Biblica,Inc.® Used by permission. All rights reserved worldwide.
"Scripture taken from the New King James Version®. Copyright © 1982 by Thomas Nelson, Inc. Used by permission. All rights reserved."
Scripture quotations marked (NLT) are taken from the Holy Bible, New Living Translation, copyright © 1996, 2004, 2007, by Tyndale House Foundation. Used by permission of Tyndale House Publishers, Inc., Carol Stream, Illinois 60188. All rights reserved.
Scripture quotations marked TPT are from The Passion Translation®. Copyright © 2017, 2018 by Passion & Fire Ministries, Inc. Used by permission. All rights reserved. ThePassionTranslation.com.
Complete Jewish Bible (CJB) Copyright © 1998 by David H. Stern. All rights reserved. No portion of this book may be reproduced, stored in a retrieval system, or transmitted in any form or by any means without prior written permission of the publisher.
NET Scripture quoted by permission. Quotations designated (NET) are from the NET Bible® copyright ©1996, 2019 by Biblical Studies Press, L.L.C. http://netbible.com. All rights reserved.
Amplified Bible, Classic Edition. Works using Amplified Bible, Classic Edition quotations must include one of the following copyright notices (whichever one is most appropriate): 1. Scripture taken from the Amplified Bible, Copyright © 1954, 1958, 1962, 1964, 1965, 1987 by The Lockman Foundation. Used by permission
The Holy Bible, Modern English Version Copyright © 2014 by Military Bible Association. All rights reserved.
Scripture quotations marked CSB are been taken from the Christian Standard Bible®, Copyright © 2017 by Holman Bible Publishers. Used by permission. Christian Standard Bible•, and CSB® are federally registered trademarks of Holman Bible Publishers.
Scripture quotations are from the Holy Bible, Evangelical Heritage Version® (EHV®) © 2019 Wartburg Project, Inc. All rights reserved. Used by permission.
WEB: World English Bible – Public Domain
KJV: King James Version – Public Domain
ASV: American Standard Version – Public Domain

Cover by: April Robinson, Graphic Artist
Text Design: Lisa Simpson
SimpsonProductions.net

Contents

Foreword 5

1 Who is Jesus Christ of Nazareth? 7
2 The Birth of Jesus 15
3 Political and Religious Climate in Jesus' Day 39
4 The Boyhood of Jesus 47
5 The Judean Ministry – The Year of Obscurity 51
6 The Beginning of Jesus' Galilean Ministry 71
7 Parables of the Kingdom of God 111
8 Sailing to the Land of the Gadarenes 119
9 Jairus, a Ruler of the Synagogue 125
10 Jesus in Jerusalem at Bethesda 131
11 Jesus Feeding the 5,000 135
12 Jesus' Perean Ministry 145
13 Jesus' Coming into the Land of Judea 153
14 Parables of Judgment and the Destruction of Jerusalem 181
15 Jesus Anointed for Burial 187
16 Preparation for Passover 191
17 The Passion of Christ 209
18 The Resurrection 233
19 The Ascension 243

Foreword

More books have been written on the life of Jesus Christ than on any other person in history, and yet the life of Christ is so vast, so marvelous that there is no way to measure the value of his person or weigh the results of his deeds. The immeasurability of his life is best described by the Apostle John when he wrote, "…there are also many other things which Jesus did, the which, if they should be written every one, I suppose that even the world itself could not contain the books that should be written, Amen" (Jn. 21:25).

The purpose of this book is to look at the life of Jesus of Nazareth in three primary ways. First, we will look at his mission and purpose as prophetic fulfillment of Old Testament prophecies. Second, we will review his life from birth to ascension, focusing on the chronological sequence of his travels and ministry. Third, we will review his primary teachings to the multitudes and his disciples as they are now handed down to us in scripture for our learning and advancement.

We will follow the three and one-half years of the ministry of Jesus beginning with his water baptism by John the Baptist, his temptation in the wilderness, and the Judean, Galilean, and Perean ministries that followed.

We will look at the date of the birth of Jesus and how Daniel accurately prophesied it to the exact year when Jesus would first enter the Temple as the Messiah.

We will look at the coming of the Kingdom of God and the resulting ministry by the Holy Spirit to enlarge the Kingdom through the Church to the ends of the earth.

Come with me as we take a verse-by-verse journey through the most exciting collection of books and letters ever written, discovering as we do the love of God for humanity and his eternal purpose for inexpressible joy and life for all who believe.

Chapter 1

Who Is Jesus Christ of Nazareth?

Jesus is God. He is equal with God. He is the eternal Word of God who created all things. Referring to Jesus, John writes, "In the beginning was the Word, and the Word was with God, and the Word was God. The same was in the beginning with God. All things were made by him; and without him was not any thing made that was made" (Jn. 1:1-3).

This same Word that made all things became man. John continues, saying, "And the Word was made flesh, and dwelt among us (and we beheld his glory, the glory as of the only begotten of the Father,) full of grace and truth" (Jn. 1:14)

The following scriptures show us that God created all things by Jesus Christ.

"And to make all men see what is the fellowship of the mystery, which from the beginning of the world hath been hid in God, who created all things by Jesus Christ:" (Eph. 3:9)

"For by him were all things created, that are in heaven, and that are in earth, visible and invisible, whether they be thrones or dominions, or principalities, or powers: all things were created by him, and for him" (Col. 1:16)

"Hath in these last days spoken unto us by his Son, whom he hath appointed heir of all things, by whom also he made the worlds;" (Heb. 1:2)

These scriptures reveal the Deity of Jesus Christ. He is God and is both equal with God and preexistent as the eternal Son of the eternal Father. When Paul writes to the Philippian Church, he shows them that Jesus, when he was in the "form" of God, was equal with God (Phil. 2:6). Jesus himself declared this preexistence when he informed the Jews that he lived before Abraham (Jn. 8:58), and when he prayed before his betrayal, he asked his Father to glorify him with the glory he had with him before the world existed (Jn. 17:5).

Although the word trinity is not found in the scriptures, the concept of a triune God is seen in the function of the Godhead (Acts 17:29; Rom. 1:20; Col. 2:9). God the Father, God the Son, and God the Holy Spirit are equal and unified in purpose and performance. It wasn't until the incarnation of the eternal Word of God (the Son) that the triune character of God was clearly revealed.

One of the clearest examples of the trinity is at the water baptism of Jesus. John the Baptist baptizes Jesus, the Son of God, in water. As Jesus comes up, out of the water, the heavens are opened and the Spirit of God descends from heaven and anoints and remains upon

Jesus as God the Father speaks from Heaven, "This is my beloved Son, in whom I am well pleased" (Mt. 3:16,17). The mystery of the trinity is not so much that the one and true living God is expressed in three persons, but that the Son of God would willingly become the Son of man, a man (spirit, soul, and body), born at a point in time with all the limitations of man and yet being the Creator of all things. This self-limitation would give Jesus the experience of being "human" but would also give man the living example of how God created man to live as God's image, free from sin and walking in dominion.

Jesus made clear the purpose of his coming. It was to fulfill the law (Mt. 5:17), to receive the judgment required for man's sin (Mt. 26:28), and to give us abundant and eternal life (Jn. 10:10). Jesus fulfilled every aspect of the law God required of man for righteousness. It was impossible for man to keep the law; therefore, Jesus came as our representative (intercessor) before God. He lived in sinless perfection, possessing the righteousness of God. Jesus then took man's place in judgment as the perfect, sinless sacrifice, to fulfill the righteous judgment of God upon sin. He then freely gives all who come to him the gift of righteousness, forgiving our sin and imparting to us his eternal and abundant life.

We have briefly looked at the deity of Jesus, but we now want to look at the humanity of Jesus. As believers, we readily accept the fact that Jesus is God, eternal and almighty. Because of our reverence for Jesus as God, we sometimes miss the reality of the humanity of Jesus as the scriptures describe him.

Paul reveals to us, through his letter to the Philippians, that Jesus "made himself of no reputation". The Amplified translation puts it like this, "But stripped Himself [of all privileges and rightful dignity], so as to assume the guise of a servant (slave), in that He became like men *and* was born a human being" (Phil. 2:7 AMP). Jesus was born a man with a human spirit, soul, and body. The man Jesus entered this world like every other person, born of a woman. Paul tells us, "But when the fullness of time was come, God sent forth his Son, made of a woman, made under the law" (Gal. 4:4)

There were many reasons that required Jesus to be human. The title he used to refer to himself, most often was the son of man, "Whom do men say that I the Son of man am?" (Mt. 16:13).

God had made man in his image and likeness and gave man authority and dominion over all things God had created (Gen. 1:26-28; Heb. 2:8). Man handed his God-given authority over to the devil when he obeyed the devil's voice and disobeyed God's command (Lk. 4:6; Rom. 6:16). Adam (man) came under the subjugation of sin by yielding to Satan, the original sinner (1 Jn. 3:8). Because Jesus was born, a human without sin, he can execute judgment as a man because he is the Son of man (Jn. 5:27).

In his "humanity" Jesus experienced the same limitations every person experiences:

He hungered (Mt. 4:2).

He experienced thirst (Jn. 19:28).

He became weary (Jn. 4:6).

He slept (Mt. 8:24).

He sorrowed (Jn. 11:35; Mt. 26:38).

He suffered and died (Jn. 19:23, 30).

The scripture declares that he was, "touched with the feeling of our infirmities" (Heb. 4:15). People have a tendency to believe they are suffering a trauma or injustice that is unique to them that nobody knows how they feel or the pain or sorrow or suffering they have experienced. But the Word of God declares that Jesus suffered, was tempted, and experienced everything mankind has endured.

Here are a few of the common experiences we may fail to recognize in Jesus' human experience. He was part of a blended family. The household Jesus lived in for many years was shared with his stepfather Joseph and four half-brothers and several half-sisters (Mt. 13:55,56). Jesus' family began when he was born of Mary after Joseph took her to be his wife even though she was already pregnant (Mt. 1:18-25). The stigma of Jesus being born out of wedlock followed him into his adult years (Jn. 8:41).

Jesus experienced the death of a beloved family member sometime between the age of 12 years and 30 years. We know this to be true because Joseph, a good man, who would never abandon his family, is never mentioned again after the family's visit to Jerusalem when Jesus was 12 years of age (Lk. 2:41-52).

Jesus experienced the rejection and misunderstanding of his brothers when he left the responsibilities of his family at 30 years of age to fulfill the purpose of his Heavenly Father. His brothers did not believe he was the Messiah (Christ), but that he had lost his mind (Jn. 7:2-5; Mk. 3:21).

Jesus experienced the temptation to remain in a very successful business instead of leaving it all behind to fulfill the ministry God had called him to complete. He left his home with no visible material support but trusted his Heavenly Father would provide for him.

Jesus' humanity was not symbolic but complete in every aspect. He suffered all the things people experience, and on the cross, he carried both the sins of the world and the judgment of those sins, the curse of every sickness and disease and the rejection of God as well as the rejection of man. Jesus knows the problems and pains of every human being. He is truly "touched" with our weakness and is the faithful and merciful High Priest who understands us perfectly.

We have observed the Deity of Jesus as Creator of all things. We have looked at the humanity of Jesus as a man, born of a woman, born under the law and with all the limitations and sufferings man experiences. Now we want to look at Jesus as the Christ, the Messiah, the Anointed One who would save mankind and destroy the works of the devil.

The Hebrew term translated "Messiah" and the Greek term "Christ" carries the same meaning, which is, anointing or the anointed one. Jesus is the Messiah, the Christ, the Anointed One. Acts 10:38 tells us that "God anointed Jesus of Nazareth with the Holy Ghost and with power: who went about doing good, and healing all that were oppressed of the devil; for God was with him." Christ is not Jesus' last name, but rather it is his title. He is Jesus, the Christ.

When did Jesus become "the Christ"? Some believe that Jesus was born "the Christ" because Matthew's gospel states that King Herod demanded that the scribes tell him where the Christ was to be born according to the scriptures (Mt. 2:4). This reference to the birth of Christ was simply identifying where, according to the prophets, the one promised by God would be born. Remembering the New Testament was written several decades after the birth, ministry, death, and resurrection of Jesus, we know the writers were not writing about the events as they happened but looking back on events that had transpired years before. Jesus, born the only begotten Son of God as well as the Creator of all things, had to grow physically and mentally, subject to all the experiences every child, teenager, and young adult experienced. He fulfilled all of the demands and requirements of the Law of Moses (Mt. 5:17). His "anointing" would fulfill all of the prophetic promises that the Messiah would accomplish as Prophet, Priest, and King.

The Christ would be a "Prophet" like Moses (Jn. 6:14; Deut. 18:15). He would be the eternal High Priest (Heb. 4:14) and King who would rule forever (Lk. 1:31-33). He fulfilled all the scriptural requirements for these titles.

Jesus as Prophet fulfilled all of the Law of Moses without sin. As the Prophet, he exactly expressed the will of God to the people, not just by the words he spoke, but by his very presence, for he himself was the Logos (living Word). His message was not limited to words but his works and person gave an exact revelation of God in every way. Jesus was the "brightness of His [God's] glory and the express image of His [God's] person" (Heb. 1:1-3).

The age requirement for a priest was 30 years. Jesus did not begin his ministry until he was 30 years of age. His priesthood was not of the Old Testament kind that was temporary, requiring daily, seasonal, and yearly sacrifices as those offered by the priests of the family of Aaron. Jesus was the eternal high priest after the order of Melchisedec (Heb. 4:14; 6:20).

Melchisedec was seen meeting Abraham when he returned from defeating Chedorlaomer and the kings that were with him (Gen. 14:18). He is called the priest of the most high God, and he blessed Abraham. This may describe the time Jesus mentioned in John 8:56, "Your father Abraham rejoiced to see my day; and he saw it and was glad." The Jews, in astonishment said to him, "You are not yet fifty years old, and have you seen Abraham? (Jn. 8:57) But, Jesus said to them, "Verily, verily, I say unto you, Before Abraham was, I am." (Jn. 8:58). This answer Jesus gave to the Jews revealed him as the "I AM, THAT I AM", the name God called himself when Moses asked his name in Exodus 3:14. Here Jesus shows his presence in Abraham's day and the nature of his eternal, high priesthood as Melchisedec, the "King of righteousness" and "King of Salem" (which means "King of peace"), "without father, without mother, without descent, having neither beginning of days, nor end of life; but made like unto the Son of God; abides a priest continually" (Heb. 7:1-3).

We see this eternal high priest is also a king. Jesus, as the Christ (anointed one) fulfilling the office of Prophet, Priest, and King is anointed with the Holy Spirit and Power (Acts. 10:38). He was born the eternal Son of God who would perfectly fulfill all the requirements of the Law. The prophets of the Old Testament uttered the perfect will of God as they spoke under the inspiration given them by the Holy Spirit even though they themselves were flawed and imperfect vessels. As Prophet Jesus brought the Word of God to the people not only with words but every aspect of his life revealed the love and will of God the Father. Jesus could therefore say to Philip, "…he that has seen me has seen the Father…" (Jn. 14:9). This perfect Prophet both spoke and gave demonstration of the perfect will of God. As the eternal High Priest, he offered himself as the "one sacrifice for sins forever", and then "sat down at the right hand of God" (Heb. 10:10-12). There he is enthroned forever as the eternal "KING OF KINGS, AND LORD OF LORDS" (Rev. 19:16).

Jesus began this work as Prophet, Priest, and King when he was anointed with the Holy Spirit at his baptism in the Jordan River. Here he became "the Christ" (the anointed one), empowered by the Spirit of God to bring God's word to the people.

CHAPTER 2

The Birth of Jesus

The majority of world governments and international businesses date legal and official documents using the calendar that recognizes the birth of our Lord Jesus Christ. His birth marked forever the measurement of time in human history. Christmas celebrations are reminders of his advent in the town of Bethlehem, born of a virgin and laid in a manger. His arrival marked the fullness of time (Gal. 4:4). His accomplishment would change forever man's relationship with God.

The conception and birth of Jesus was unlike any other. The promise of man's deliverance from sin and corresponding defeat of the devil was first proclaimed by God in the Book of Genesis (Gen. 3:15). The "seed" of the woman would crush the head (authority) of the serpent (devil) and in the process would be "bruised" himself.

The question is, "How can there be a seed of a woman? The phrase is in contradiction to biology. The woman does not carry the seed, the man does; therefore, how can there be a seed of the woman?

We know that Adam is the fountainhead of all humanity. Every person born into this world has come through the lineage of Adam. Man's inheritance in Adam is sin (Rom. 5:12). Adam's seed carries more than just physical DNA. It also carries the nature of Adam, which is sin. "In Adam all die" (1 Cor. 15:22; Eph. 2:1-3).

But Jesus was not born of Adam. Mary's conception was not of man but of God (Lk. 1:34,35). A virgin was to give birth to the Son of God (Isa. 7:14). Jesus possessed the divine nature, not the inherited sin nature of man. He was born, not of the corruptible seed of man, but of the incorruptible seed of the Word of God (Jn. 1:1,14).

Jesus is referred to as the "second man", in Paul's letter to the Corinthians (1 Cor. 15:47). Both in Matthew's gospel and Luke's we can find the genealogy of Joseph and Mary respectively. Just common knowledge tells us that many people were born between Adam and Jesus, so how can Jesus be referred to as the "second man"?

Adam was made in the "image and likeness of God" (Gen. 1:26). He carried that image until sin entered his life and the image of God was marred. Sin separated Adam and God. Apart from God, man's sin nature distorted God's image. Jesus was not born of man's seed, but God's. He perfectly displayed the image and likeness of God (Heb. 1:2-3; Jn. 14:9-10). Jesus was the "second man" to carry God's image; however the term "second" implies that there could be a third, fourth and so on. Such is the purpose of God that Jesus would be the "first-born" of many brethren (Rom. 8:29).

Jesus is also referred to as the "last Adam" (1 Cor. 15:45). As Adam, the first man, was the fountainhead of all humanity who were made in his image and likeness, so Jesus is the "last Adam", i.e. the fountainhead of mankind made in the image and likeness of God.

There will be no more "Adams" to propagate their images; Jesus is the last.

When we are born of the Spirit of God, we are a brand-new creation that never existed before (2 Cor. 5:17). Many people have a hard time understanding the new birth. Nicodemus, a high-ranking member of the supreme court of Israel, heard Jesus say that people must be born again to see the kingdom of God, and Nicodemus answered, "How can these things be?" (Jn. 3:9). Jesus' reply should bring to us a better understanding of the new birth, He said, "That which is born of the flesh is flesh; and that which is born of the Spirit is spirit" (Jn. 3:6).

When we are "born-again," our body remains the same and our soul (mind, will, and emotions) is unchanged except for some new information. It is our spirit that is made brand new. Our spirit is born of the Holy Spirit of God, and we become the "righteousness of God" in Christ Jesus (2 Cor. 5:21). We are now righteous, not because of what we do or don't do, but because of what Jesus did for us. He took our sin, and we "receive" his righteousness. That is why people who are born-again can still act like the world (their natural man) because they are not living out of the spirit (who they really are 1 Cor. 3:1-3). The will of God is for all believers to "grow up" in Christ, to present their bodies for God's purpose and to "renew" their minds (Rom. 12:1,2), to know his will and to walk out their faith so others can look at them and see God's image. Jesus is the "firstborn of many brethren" and the "last Adam," the fountainhead of a new race of people from every tongue, tribe, kindred, and nation (Rev. 7:9) who now have been made again in the image and likeness of God.

Jesus' earthly parents were both of the royal line of king David. Many Old Testament prophecies declare the Messiah would come through the seed of David (Ps. 89:3,4, 34,37). Both the Gospel of Matthew and the Gospel of Luke reveal the lineage of Jesus according to the flesh. Luke's account (Lk. 3:23-38) shows Mary's lineage comes through king David. Matthew's account shows Joseph's lineage, although different, also comes through king David. The scriptures show that Joseph had nothing to do with the birth of Jesus for Mary was impregnated by the Holy Spirit and not by a man. So why would Matthew's gospel show Joseph's lineage?

Joseph's lineage was "cursed" as he was a descendant of king Jechonias who is also referred to as Jeconiah, Jehoiachin, and Coniah. Jechonias was an evil king of Judah resulting in the prophet Jeremiah's announcement that God told him, "Write ye this man childless, a man that shall not prosper in his days: for no man of his seed shall prosper, sitting upon the throne of David, and ruling any more in Judah" (Jer. 22:28-30). Through this prophetic word, we see that neither Joseph nor his "seed" could ever sit as king on the throne of David. But, Jesus was not of Joseph but was the Son of God and yet of the lineage of king David through his mother Mary.

JOHN THE BAPTIST IS BORN

The story of John the Baptist begins with an angelic visitation to a priest named Zacharias (Lk. 1:5). Although Zacharias and his wife Elisabeth were honorable before the Lord, Elisabeth was barren and they both were now old. Elisabeth had carried the shame of being childless. According to the Law of Moses, those who followed the Lord and observed to do his word would be fruitful. A wife that was barren was suspected of displeasing God, so Elisabeth would have been looked on by her peers as cursed for some sin of hers or her family's. But, God saw her differently, describing her and her husband as "righteous before God, walking in all the commandments and ordinances of the Lord blameless "(Lk. 1:6). God's plan for this couple would not only erase the shame of barrenness but would bring forth a son that would be known as the greatest prophet ever born (Lk. 7:28).

There were some 20,000 priests in Judea in those days, so those chosen to fulfill a service in the Temple were selected by lots. Zacharias was chosen to offer the incense on the golden altar before the veil in the Holy Place during the morning and evening sacrifices. This was a great honor and not one in which every priest could participate. It is not known if Zacharias had ever been chosen before for such a service, so this may have been the first time he ever participated in actually serving in the Holy Place. To enter the Holy Place with a hot coal from the brazen altar and place that coal on the golden altar of incense in front of the veil and sprinkle incense on that coal would create a fragrant smoke that would filter within the veil. This smoke was representative of the prayers of the people then praying in the outer court each morning and evening (Lk. 1:10). It was during this time at the golden altar that the angel Gabriel appeared to Zacharias and said, "Fear not, Zacharias: for your prayer is heard; and your wife Elisabeth shall bear you a son, and you shall call his name John" (Lk. 1:13). The angel continued to tell Zacharias about this child and his mission to announce the coming of the Messiah.

It is interesting to note that the angel announced this good news as an answer to Zacharias' prayer for his wife Elisabeth to bear a son. The reaction of Zacharias to this news shows us this prayer had been prayed many years earlier. He had obviously given up the idea that he and his wife would ever have a child, for they were now both advanced in years.

Zacharias' response to the angel, "Whereby shall I know this?" brought both a word of rebuke and a sign, but not likely the sign, he wanted to see. The angel identified himself as Gabriel who stands in the presence of God. Gabriel had visited Daniel to bring him God's answer to his prayer and to cause Daniel to understand the vision he had received (Dan. 8:16; 9:21). This same mighty angel was bringing good news and an important message to this aged priest. Zacharias' unbelief was met with a sign that caused him to be dumb, unable to speak, until the promised child had been born.

After Zacharias' ministry in the Temple was completed, he returned home, and soon Elisabeth conceived. She rejoiced that God had visited her and that soon her reproach would be removed with the birth of her son (Lk. 1:24).

It was in Elisabeth's sixth month of pregnancy that her young cousin Mary came to visit her. Mary already knew of her cousin's pregnancy, for the angel Gabriel had also visited this young girl in her native village of Nazareth. Gabriel's announcement to Mary as God's chosen vessel to bear the Son of God was followed with the information about Elisabeth's miracle. Mary quickly left Nazareth in Galilee and traveled the 60 miles south to the Judean hill country. There is no indication that Mary traveled with others, but apparently made the trip alone, although such travel was neither safe nor convenient. Arriving at the home of the aged couple, Mary was greeted with a prophetic word from Elisabeth. As Mary knocked at the door, raising her voice to greet her distant relative, the Holy Spirit filled Elisabeth and her yet unborn baby, and Elisabeth began to speak by the Spirit things that only Mary could have known (Lk. 1:41-45). Elisabeth ended her speaking and Mary began to prophesy of her future and God's faithfulness to fulfill his promises to Abraham and his seed. Mary remained with Zacharias and Elisabeth until the birth of John. They no doubt passed the final days of Elisabeth's pregnancy in great anticipation and wonder about the future of their children.

At the circumcision of the baby his name John was made official. Elisabeth encountered much opposition about the naming of the baby as the other relatives who came to rejoice at his birth called him Zacharias after his father. Elisabeth insisted he be named John as the angel had instructed her husband in the Temple. When the people motioned to Zacharias about the decision he wrote on a tablet, "His name is John" (Lk. 1:63). With that Zacharias was suddenly able to speak and began to prophesy as he too was filled with the Holy Spirit. He spoke of the promises of God to his people and the part this child would play in preparing the way for the coming Messiah.

The Ministry of John the Baptist

Both Isaiah and Malachi had prophesied regarding the ministry of John the Baptist many centuries before John was ever born (Isa. 40:3-5; Mal. 3:1). Matthew confirms that the ministry of John is indeed the fulfillment of Isaiah's prophesy of the one crying in the wilderness (Mt. 3:1-3). But why was John in the wilderness in the first place? The answer likely involves a Jewish sect known as the Essenes. This ascetic group became well known as their number in John's day exceeded 4,000. They lived in the desert along the banks of the Jordan River just north of the Dead Sea. Being disillusioned with the corrupt dealings of the Jewish leadership, the Essenes did not offer sacrifices or visit the Temple. They denied themselves most of the comforts of life and lived in the strictest observance of religious duties. Men and women remained separated except on the Sabbath day when they came together to worship and eat coarse bread and salt. Few married, but they perpetuated their sect by taking in orphan children. It was the Essenes who were responsible for the Dead Sea scrolls.

It is surmised that John, being born to elderly parents, was probably orphaned at a young age. The fact that he did not follow his father into the priesthood and was living in the desert along the banks of the Jordan and dressed in the style of the Essenes, would lead us to believe he was associated with this group.

John, the Forerunner of Christ, Came in the Spirit of Elijah.

So who was John the Baptist? The Scriptures identify him as the forerunner, the one who went before the Messiah to announce his arrival and to turn the hearts of the people back to God. John is first described by the prophet Isaiah as, "The voice of him that cries in the wilderness, Prepare the way of the Lord make straight in the desert a highway for our God" (Isa. 40:3).

Here in Isaiah we have a picture of the servant that goes before the king's chariot to clear the road of every obstacle. The rocks and litter are moved out of the way, and the potholes are filled in so the road will provide a smooth ride for the king's chariot and its royal passengers. Isaiah greatly exaggerates this metaphor, filling in every valley and making every mountain and hill a level place. This "voice in the wilderness" is not preparing the way for an earthly king but a heavenly one. The voice of this messenger is to reveal the glory of God and remind both Zion and Jerusalem of the good tidings of the arrival of the promised Messiah.

The prophet Malachi also promises the coming of Elijah the prophet who will precede the "day of the Lord" to "turn the heart of the fathers to the children, and the heart of the children to their fathers..." (Mal. 4:5,6)

Both Isaiah and Malachi describe the work of the forerunner who was revealed by the angel Gabriel to Zacharias, the father of John. Speaking of John, Gabriel told Zacharias, "he shall go before him[the Messiah] in the spirit and power of Elias [Elijah]" (Lk. 1:17). John himself said he was not the prophet Elijah but was "the voice of one crying in the wilderness...as said the prophet Esaias [Isaiah]" (Jn. 1:21,22).

When Jesus was asked about John, he said John the Baptist was the messenger who went ahead to prepared the way and was the "Elias" [Elijah], who was to come (Mt. 11:9-14). Jesus was not referring to John as the reincarnation of Elijah the prophet, but as Malachi and Gabriel declared, he would come in the spirit and power of Elijah. Elijah was commissioned by God to anoint Hazael to be king over Syria and Jehu to be king over Israel and to anoint Elisha as a prophet to take his place (1 Kings 19:15,16). As a prophet, even as the greatest prophet of the Old Testament (Mt. 11:11), John was to announce the arrival and prepare the way for Jesus as both King and Prophet (Jn. 6:14,15; Deut. 18:15,18; Lk. 1:32,33).

Dating the Birth of Jesus

Jesus was born in Bethlehem (house of bread). The name of the town is befitting his birth for Jesus said, "I am the bread of life" (Jn. 6:35). We celebrate the birth of Jesus on December 25th for a number of different reasons. The 4th Century Church experienced a great number of pagan converts entering the Church whose lives and cultures revolved around their pagan festivals. In an attempt to give Christian meaning to pagan festivals the Church tried to find suitable substitutes such as Easter (the spring festival to the pagan goddess Ishtar) and make it a celebration of the resurrection of Christ. Likewise, the celebration of the birth of the Roman Unconquered Sun god on December 25th was changed to the celebration of the birth of the Son of God, the source of Light and Salvation. (Eerdmans' Handbook to the History of Christianity, pg. 131).

Although December the 25th became the official day of celebration for the birth of Christ, was he actually born that late in the year? To determine the date of the birth of Jesus we need to look at prophetic references, Church history, and the timeline recorded in the gospels. Without going into great detail, we can see in John's gospel three specific Feasts of Passover mentioned (Jn. 2:13, 6:4, 11:55). We know Jesus was crucified on that third Passover.

Prior to the first Passover mentioned, Jesus had left Nazareth, traveled to the Jordan River where John was baptizing, spent 40 days in the Perean wilderness, returned to John at Jordan, recruited six disciples, traveled some 60 miles north to Cana where he attended a wedding and performed the first miracle and traveled with his mother and brothers to Capernaum before heading to Jerusalem to attend his first Feast of Passover as the Christ (Anointed One). The time required to accomplish all of these events must have been, at least, several months or more.

According to "The Chronological Bible" the first Passover mentioned in John 2 was in the year A.D. 27. There is no mention of the Passover for year A.D. 28 in either John's gospel or the synoptics so the next Passover in John 6 was in A.D. 29 and then the last Passover, also being the crucifixion, was in A.D. 30.

Historically, the time span for the ministry of Jesus was 3 ½ years. If that timeline was correct, then Jesus would have been born near the end of September or in early October if he were crucified on Passover (April) of A.D. 30. Having ministered after his baptism for 3 ½ years and dying in April, he would have been born in the early fall near the time of the combined Feast of Tabernacles, Day of Atonement, and Feast of Trumpets.

If the seven yearly feasts of Israel were all foreshadowing the life, work, and ministry of Jesus, then his birth date during one of the feasts would be very significant.

Let's look briefly at the seven feasts of Israel and how they portray Jesus the Messiah.

#1 Passover – the first feast of the Jewish year (near the beginning of April).

Jesus and his disciples celebrated the Passover after sundown at the beginning of the Passover day (the Jewish new day begins at sundown). He would be crucified that same day and die on the cross at 3:00 in the afternoon. In many New Testament references Jesus is referred to as "the Lamb of God, which takes away the sin of the world' (Jn. 1:29). Jesus is our paschal lamb/sacrifice.

#2 Feast of Unleavened Bread – The next evening following Passover is the feast of unleavened bread. This feast last seven days and only unleavened bread is to be eaten. Leaven can represent sin, and the bread eaten for seven days (seven is a number that represents perfection or completion) is without leaven. Jesus is the "bread of life" who is without sin. The Jewish unleavened bread or "matzoh" is stripped and pierced, just as Jesus' body was for us. During this feast, the bread is broken and the middle piece is hidden away (buried) and then revealed (resurrected) just as Jesus was.

#3 Feast of First Fruits – This feast is celebrated on the first day following the Sabbath after the Passover. A priest would go into the grain fields and harvest a few sheaths that had ripened early, return to the Temple and wave them before the Lord as representative of the harvest to come in 50 more days. Jesus was resurrected from the dead on the Feast of First Fruits (Sunday). He came out of the tomb (the first man born again from the dead), and with him there were others whose tombs were also opened to witness to the resurrection in Jerusalem (Mt. 27:52,53). Jesus, and those who rose with him fulfilled this Jewish feast.

#4 Feast of Pentecost – This feast is celebrated 50 days following the Feast of First Fruits. Pentecost in Greek means 50 and so Pentecost is the 50th day following the first fruits and this feast celebrates harvest time. The priest goes into the grain fields, which are now fully ripened, and harvests some of the grain. He returns and grinds the grain into meal and bakes two loaves of bread. He then stands before the Temple and waves the two loaves before the Lord, signifying that God's promise of harvest has been fulfilled. It was on the Feast of Pentecost that the Holy Spirit was given to the Church and the 120 were baptized in the Holy Spirit. That day Peter, being filled with the Holy Spirit, preached and a harvest of 3,000 people in Jerusalem were born again into the Kingdom of God (Acts 2).

#5 Feast of Trumpets – This feast occurred in the fall of the year, usually in September. It was in the "seventh month, in the first day of the month" (Lev. 23:24). The trumpets would sound, and the people would gather together at the Temple. This first day of Tishri is the civil New Year's Day (although it is the first day of the seventh month in the ecclesiastical year). Trumpets are common symbols of announcing the presence of the Lord and the people assembling together before Him (Ex. 19:16). In Revelation there are seven angels with seven trumpets, and they announce different events taking place in the earth, but when the seventh angel blows the trumpet a declaration is made that, "the kingdoms of this world are become the kingdoms of our Lord and of his Christ: and he shall reign for ever and ever" (Rev. 11:15). Jesus, our king, was raised from the dead, ascended into heaven and is seated at the right hand of Him who sits on the throne. He rules and reigns as King of kings and Lord of lords. The trumpets announce a new year and a new king. It is only 10 days after the Feast of Trumpets that the next feast is celebrated.

#6 Day of Atonement - This feast was on the tenth day of Tishri and was the only day of the year the High Priest could enter the Most Holy Place, within the veil where the ark of the covenant and the glory of the presence of the Lord was. The purpose of the High Priest entering the Most Holy Place was to sprinkle the blood of the sacrifice upon the mercy seat, which represented the throne of God. We know Jesus is our High Priest, and he entered into Heaven, and before the throne of God he sprinkled his own blood after obtaining eternal redemption for us (Heb. 9:11,12). It was also on the Day of Atonement that every 50 years the Jubilee was announced to the nation. On that day, after the high priest came out of the Most Holy Place, the trumpets would begin to sound throughout the land declaring that Jubilee had come and everyone would be released from bondage and debt and restored to their rightful inheritance. Jesus had announced the anointing of the Holy Spirit upon him was to fulfill the "acceptable day of the Lord" – the Jubilee (Lk. 4:18-21). Jesus fulfilled the work of the High Priest and the trumpets announced our redemption by His sacrifice.

#7 Feast of Tabernacles – This feast was celebrated on the 15th day of Tishri, just five days after the Day of Atonement (Lev. 23:34,42,43). The children of Israel were to build shelters outside of their homes and commemorate God's sheltering them when they wandered in the desert. God's presence (tabernacle) among the nation in a pillar of fire and pillar of cloud covered them and protected them from the harsh conditions, so Jesus arrived as Emmanuel ("God with us" Mt. 1:23). His completed work of redemption was realized when Jesus and the Father came to dwell in believers in the person of the Holy Spirit (Jn. 14:16, 23). The fulfillment of this feast can be seen when "He who sits on the throne shall spread His Tabernacle over them" (Rev. 7:15 WEB).

We see in these Jewish festivals, different aspects of the ministry of Jesus and how these Old Covenant rituals were fulfilled in the person and work of Jesus Christ. If his birth took place during the Feast of Tabernacles then the very name of Emmanuel, meaning "God with us," is more than coincidental, and since the Day of Atonement is also during the Feast of Tabernacles, his birth as the Lamb of God to be sacrificed to fulfill the promise of Jubilee is even more significant.

When Jesus left the family home and business in Nazareth, he was thirty years of age (Lk. 3:23). If his birthday was during the Feast of Tabernacles, then his birth date would be in September in 5 B.C. according to our calendar. But why would 5 B.C. (B.C. referring to before the birth of Christ) be accurate if our calendar is supposed to begin with the birth of Christ as the dividing point in history?

In the sixth century A.D. the pope commissioned a monk named Dionysius Exiguus to create a new calendar, to date all events from the birth of Christ. At this time all things were dated from the inception of the city of Rome, so Dionysius produced a new calendar and determined the birth of Christ to be in the Roman year 754 Anno Urbis. His calculations were obviously incorrect because of one, very well documented event, the death of Herod the Great in 750 Anno Urbis.

Herod the Great was very much alive at the birth of Jesus for the Magi came to him at the palace in Jerusalem having followed the star to find the new king of Israel. It was king Herod who ordered the death of all male infants of two years old and younger in order to destroy the newborn king. Therefore, Jesus must have been born prior to Herod's death in 750. It is well documented that Herod the Great died on March 13th in 750 Anno Urbis. If Jesus were born during the last Jewish feast prior to Herod's death, then he would have been born in September of 5 B.C. according to the calendar of Dionysius.

Is this date of 5 B.C. validated in any other scriptures? Let's look at the prophecy from the Book of Daniel.

> "Seventy weeks (sevens) are determined for your people and for your holy city, to finish the transgression, to make an end of sins, to make reconciliation for iniquity, to bring in everlasting righteousness, to seal up vision and prophecy, And to anoint the Most Holy. "Know therefore and understand, *that* from the going forth of the command to restore and build Jerusalem until Messiah the Prince, *There shall be* seven weeks (sevens) and sixty-two weeks (sevens); The Street shall be built again, and the wall, even in troublesome times. "And after the sixty-two weeks (sevens) Messiah shall be cut off, but not for Himself; and the people of the prince who is to come shall destroy the city and the sanctuary. The end of it *shall be* with a flood, and till the end of the war desolations are determined. Then he shall confirm a covenant with many for

one week (seven); but in the middle of the week (seven) He shall bring an end to sacrifice and offering. And on the wing of abominations shall be one who makes desolate, even until the consummation, which is determined, is poured out on the desolate" (Dan. 9:24-27 NKJV).

This scripture gives us specific dates of when the Messiah (Anointed One) would appear. Daniel declares a time period of 490 years that are determined to fulfill many things that only Jesus could have accomplished. Daniel also tells when this 490-year period would begin, He writes, "That from the going forth of the command to restore and build Jerusalem until Messiah the Prince, would be 483 years" (69 weeks/sevens). According to the Chronological Bible the command given by the Persian King Artaxerxes for the Jewish exiles to return and rebuild the city of Jerusalem under Ezra was 458 B.C. (this same date is given in many historical references. The first exiles returned earlier under Zerubbabel by decree of king Cyrus. They were to rebuild the Temple. The second return of exiles was under Ezra and Nehemiah who were to rebuild the city (it's walls and gates). Adding 483 years to the year of the command to rebuild Jerusalem (458 B.C.) brings us to A.D. 26 (when adding remember there is no year 0). If Jesus was 30 years old when he left Nazareth and was baptized in the Jordan River by John the Baptist and was also anointed by the Holy Spirit (Mt. 3:16) in A.D. 26 then 30 years prior would be 5 B.C. The exact year determined by the closest Jewish festival preceding King Herod's death.

There are other scriptures to corroborate this same date. For example, Daniel declares that the Messiah will confirm a covenant with many for one week (seven years) but in the middle of the week (3 ½ years) he shall bring an end to sacrifice and offering. Jesus' 3-½ year ministry came to an end when he was crucified and the veil of the Temple was torn from the top to the bottom. There would be no more animal sacrifices. Jesus had accomplished the fulfillment of all sacrifices. The priests may have sewed the divided veil in the Temple to resume their daily sacrifices, but as far as God was concerned, the final sacrifice had been offered.

Jesus also testified that the destruction of the city of Jerusalem and the Temple would take place within that generation (40 years). Jesus was crucified and resurrected in A.D. 30, and 40 years later the Roman General Titus marched on the city of Jerusalem and burned the city and destroyed the Temple in A.D. 70.

In fact, we have several scriptural references to the approximate birth date of Jesus in September 5 B.C.

Events Surrounding the Birth of Jesus (Lk. 2; Mt. 2)

The angel Gabriel visits a young girl named Mary in the small village of Nazareth in the land of Galilee. Although there is no definite record of Mary's age, it has been suggested from the oral traditions handed down for generations as well as the earliest records of Church history that Mary was a young teenage girl who became engaged to Joseph a much older man. Often marriages were arranged by families, and it would appear that both Joseph and Mary were of the same village of Nazareth. Most people would live their entire lifetime in the same village where they were born. The patriarch (father) of the family made decisions for the whole family. At the death of the patriarch, the oldest son would then take his place receiving the majority of the inheritance in order to assume the role and responsibilities of the family and the family business. Trade skills were handed down from father to son, so every male family member would remain in the family business for generations.

Joseph was known as the carpenter, a trade that included more than just woodwork, but was more of a general contractor working with wood and stone and doing a variety of construction work.

The Birth of Jesus

It has been estimated that Nazareth was a small village with a population of just over 100 residents. Here families lived together, side by side, for generations. This close community had much social strength, but no family secrets were kept secret for long.

Joseph's family and Mary's family most likely had a long history together and when Mary became a woman of age for marriage (possibly 14 or 15 years old) their long-arranged engagement would have been consummated in marriage. This engagement was a binding, legal relationship that could only be dissolved by a legal divorce. It was prior to Joseph and Mary's marriage that the angel appeared to Mary with some astounding news.

Luke tells us, "And in the sixth month [of Elisabeth's pregnancy] the angel Gabriel was sent from God unto city of Galilee, named Nazareth, To a virgin espoused to a man whose name was Joseph, of the house of David; and the virgin's name was Mary." (Lk. 1:26-28). In this encounter with the angel, Mary was told that she was "highly favored" of the Lord and would be "blessed among women." (Lk. 1:28). Gabriel goes on to explain to her that she was chosen by God to conceive in her womb and give birth to a son who would be called Jesus. Mary's response to the angel was not like the unbelief of Zacharias, which brought upon him an inability to speak, but Mary's question was only how this pregnancy would be accomplished. The angel told her that the Holy Spirit would come upon her and she would conceive and bear the Son of God. Mary's declaration reveals her trust in God and her willingness to be completely submitted to his will. "...Be it unto me according to your word" (Lk. 1:38).

It was very soon after Mary's visit by the angel, because it was still the sixth month of Elisabeth's pregnancy, that she left Nazareth to make the approximately 60-mile journey to Zacharias and Elisabeth's home in Judea. Mary stayed with Elisabeth until John was born, then returned to her home in Nazareth. In her 3-month absence her pregnancy became obvious to Joseph and the small village must have been occupied with many rumors of some illicit affair that resulted in Mary's pregnancy. It was during this time Joseph considered divorcing Mary quietly and not bringing upon her the judgment recommended by the Law of Moses, which could have resulted in her stoning at the door of her father's house (Deut. 22:21). Instead, Joseph's love for Mary was revealed in his desire to privately end their engagement, but that very night Joseph was visited in a dream by an angel who explained Mary's pregnancy was the divine plan of God to fulfill scripture and bring his Son into the world. Joseph awoke from his sleep and took Mary to be his wife as the angel had instructed him (Mt. 1:20-25).

Can you imagine the stigma Joseph, Mary, and Jesus would have to live with from those in Nazareth who would not believe their story? The reputation of Jesus as an illegitimate child followed him through his adult years (Jn. 8:41).

Caesar Augustus decreed that all subjects of the Roman Empire were to return to the city of their family linage to register for a census and pay taxes. Since both Joseph and Mary were of the lineage of David, they went to Bethlehem, the city of David, to be taxed (Lk. 2:1-5). This was a journey of nearly 60 miles and Mary, being nine months into her pregnancy, must have had a difficult time trying to walk or ride a donkey across the rocky terrain. Arriving in Bethlehem they discovered that there was no lodging for them. The crowds that traveled ahead of them surely traveled more quickly, not being slowed by a woman in her advanced pregnancy. The couple's only shelter was in the barn behind the local inn or possibly a cave where the shepherds brought the ewes that were about to birth their lambs. It was there Mary went into labor and brings forth her firstborn son, Jesus. The birth of a baby is always a time of celebration, but here Joseph and Mary were alone, without family members or friendly neighbors to adore the newborn child. But this was not just the birth of any child; it was the birth of God's own Son, and all creation would hear the celebration of heaven at the birth of Jesus.

The Birth of Jesus

An angel appears to shepherds in the field outside the town of Bethlehem. His announcement was not subtle, but was accompanied by the light of the glory of the Lord that shined all around them. The angel declared to them that the long-awaited Messiah had been born in Bethlehem and they would find him, the Savior of the world, wrapped in swaddling clothes and lying in a manger. His announcement was emphasized by the sudden appearance of a multitude of angels all praising God and declaring in unison, "Glory to God in the highest, and on earth peace, good will toward men" (Lk. 2:13,14).

I don't know if we can really grasp the magnitude of this heavenly celebration. I don't know how many a multitude of heavenly host are, but since this is the birth of God's Son, I have to believe it was not just some, but all angels and other heavenly beings celebrating the birth of Jesus. When John had the vision of heaven, he saw a multitude so large that its members could not be counted, and when Mount Zion is described in Hebrews 12:22 this heavenly city of God has an "innumerable" (too many to count) number of angels. When Jesus prayed and God the Father answered him audibly from Heaven (Jn. 12:28,29), some of the people said, "An angel spoke to him," and others said, "it thundered." If the voice of one angel could sound like thunder, what would the voices of a countless number of angels all praising God at once sound like? I imagine that all the residence of Bethlehem and Jerusalem, just two miles away, heard the thunderous praise of these angels that shook the earth as more than 4,000 years of prophesy was now fulfilled.

The angels did not make the announcement of the birth of Jesus to the religious leaders in the Temple, just a few miles away, but to shepherds, and not just any shepherds. It should be noted that the flocks of sheep that grazed in the fields surrounding Bethlehem were sacred flocks. These sheep were not raised to be sold in the market place but were only to be offered in sacrifice at the Temple. These shepherds "spread abroad" (Lk. 2:17,18), i.e. they told everyone about the encounter with the angels and what they said about the child in the manger in Bethlehem. These shepherds who were responsible to oversee the lambs for sacrifice were shown the Lamb of God, birthed in a barn among the sacred flocks.

The fact that the baby would be wrapped in swaddling clothes was a sign to the shepherds, for swaddling clothes were strips of cloth that were used to wrap the new born lambs to keep them from falling and bruising themselves. These lambs were to be free of bruises or blemishes in order to be worthy for sacrifice. How significant was this sign to the shepherds that the Savior, the Lamb of God, was born among the sacred flock and preserved for sacrifice?

A Witness to the Priests in Jerusalem

The birth of Jesus was announced to the people of Bethlehem and all the surrounding area when the celebrating angels revealed the glory of God. The shepherds hearing the message from the angels found the baby in the manger and then told everyone they met concerning the child. Then eight days later Joseph and Mary took the baby to the Temple in Jerusalem where he was circumcised and named Jesus (Jehovah saves) according to the name given to Mary by the angel Gabriel before she conceived. Now, 40 days after his birth, Mary and Joseph brought, for her purification, an offering of a turtledove and a young pigeon.

The kind of offering Joseph and Mary brought was very significant. According to the Law of Moses a woman, having given birth to a male child was to bring an offering of a lamb of the first year for a burnt offering and a young pigeon or turtledove for a sin offering to be offered by the priest (Lev. 12:6-8). Only if the couple were too poor to bring a lamb could they offer instead two turtledoves or two young pigeons. Wouldn't Joseph and Mary have brought the best possible offering they could afford? Undoubtedly, Joseph had to leave his business and travel to Bethlehem, register his household for the census, and pay taxes to Caesar. This must have depleted any savings they may have had until all that was left was the offering prescribed for the poor.

Testimony to the birth of the Messiah continues in Jerusalem when Simeon, a righteous and devout man, who was anointed by the Holy Spirit, entered the Temple just as Joseph and Mary had completed the offering for Mary's purification. He took Jesus in his arms and began to prophesy of future events concerning Jesus' redemptive work, which was to include the Gentiles, and the hardships Mary would endure as a result. Just as Simeon declared these things and then blessed Joseph, Mary, and Jesus, Anna, a prophetess, entered. She also served the Lord with fasting and prayers night and day (Lk. 2:37). Now, at a very advanced age, Anna, seeing the child, blessed the Lord and spoke to everyone in Jerusalem who were waiting for the birth of the Messiah that he had arrived.

The Visit of the Magi

After the Temple visit, Joseph and Mary returned with Jesus to Bethlehem. Joseph, by this time, had secured a house for them to live in. Sometime within the next four months, a caravan would enter the city of Jerusalem looking for the newborn king of Israel. This announcement would trouble all of Jerusalem, for Herod, the wicked "king of the Jews," had ruthlessly fought to maintain his dominion, even killing many of his own children and other family members whom he believed could threaten his reign. This parade of camels carried a priestly class of Persians who arrived in the city with great fanfare. They announced publicly that they had seen a new star from their homeland, possibly some five hundred miles east in Babylon. While we don't know specifically about the origin of these Magi, most scholars believe they were astrologers from Persia. They had seen a new star in the night skies over the land of Israel and understood this to mean that a new king had been born to rule the land.

There are many scriptural references to the meaning of the sun and moon and stars and other celestial bodies. According to Genesis, the heavenly lights were given for signs and for seasons and for days and years (1:14). In Joseph's dream, he saw the sun and moon and eleven stars bow down to him. His father understood that to mean that he and Joseph's mother and eleven brothers would one day bow to him as ruler (Gen. 37:9-11). Many prophecies speak to the judgment of nations as the destruction of the sun and stars falling from the sky, the darkness resulting from that kingdoms' collapse (Isa. 13:1-10; Ezek. 32:1-8; Mt. 24:29). Conversely, when a new star was seen, it meant that a new king or kingdom was being birthed. To these Magi (wise men), the appearance of a new star was God's announcement of the birth of a king, and since the star was over Israel, Israel must have a new king. Where would you find a king, but in the palace of that kingdom? Hence, they traveled to Jerusalem, the capital city, to enquire at the king's palace about the birth of the new king and their desire to worship him.

The term worship can carry with it reverence for God or for royalty. Since there was still a large population of Jews in Persia, these Magi may have learned from them about a coming Messiah and believed the star announced his arrival or that a son had been born to the king. Either way they traveled a long way with their treasures and servants and armed security. This parade of wealthy Magi with their huge entourage must have caused much consternation among all the people of Jerusalem.

With the inquiry at the palace, King Herod summoned the scribes to identify the city were the Messiah/King would be born. After receiving the report about Micah's prophecy (5:2) that the everlasting ruler of Israel would be born in Bethlehem of Judea, Herod pointed the wise men in the right direction and ordered them to find the child and then return to him so he too could worship the child also, for Bethlehem was only a few miles away. The searching Magi would have been unaware of Herod's devious plan to kill this infant

The Birth of Jesus

king when his location was discovered. Traveling towards Bethlehem they once again saw the star that led them to the house where Jesus was. This shows us that the star was not some asteroid or planetary alignment, but was most likely an angel of the Lord (see Rev. 1:20) for this star had not been seen for some time, and then it appeared before them and led them to the house of Joseph and Mary. Finding the child, they presented their gifts of gold, frankincense, and myrrh. These gifts were of great value and would have supplied Joseph and Mary with the necessary finances for their travel and lodging in Egypt. After the Magi had fulfilled their mission, they returned to their own country "another way," probably breaking camp early the next morning, for they had a dream that night of God warning them not to return to Herod. Not wanting a conflict with the king, they left for their own country quietly, taking a different route to avoid Jerusalem. They had fulfilled God's purpose as a witness to Herod and all of Jerusalem that the Messiah had been born and to provide, through their gifts, the necessary finances for Joseph, Mary, and Jesus as they traveled to Egypt.

Joseph also had a dream that same night instructing him to leave Bethlehem immediately and go to Egypt and live there until after the death of Herod because he would seek to kill Jesus. Joseph obeyed the angel who appeared to him in the dream and took his family and belongings and left Bethlehem before daylight to escape Herod's murderous intentions. The next morning when Herod discovered the Magi had left the area without notifying him as they were instructed, he became extremely angry and ordered his soldiers to kill all the infant male babies, up to two years of age, in Bethlehem and the surrounding region. This tragic event had been prophesied by Jeremiah the prophet over five hundred years earlier. Jeremiah wrote, "In Rama was there a voice heard, lamentation, and weeping, and great mourning, Rachel weeping for her children, refused be comforted, because they are not" (Jer. 31:15; Mt. 2:17).

Joseph returned to Israel after the death of Herod, being instructed again by an angel in a dream. This time he and his family were to reside in Galilee and dwell in Nazareth. All of these events fulfilled a series of prophetic words. The family's leaving Egypt (Mt. 2:15), and traveling to Galilee, and settling in Nazareth (Mt. 2:22,23), each of these actions and locations had been declared centuries before.

CHAPTER 3

POLITICAL AND RELIGIOUS CLIMATE IN JESUS' DAY

After the reign of King David and his son King Solomon, the kingdom of Israel was divided into two kingdoms. The northern kingdom was known as Israel, and the southern kingdom was called Judah and included the capital city of Jerusalem and the Temple. These kingdoms often warred against one another until the Assyrians conquered Israel and either killed or dispersed its inhabitants among the cities of the Assyrian empire around 721 B.C. About 135 years later the Babylonians, under the command of Nebuchadnezzar, invaded Judah and destroyed the capital city of Jerusalem and the Temple, taking many of the inhabitants into exile about 586 B.C.

During the 70 years of exile in Babylon, the Jews had no Temple in which to worship or offer sacrifices. In their quest to preserve the teachings of the Law of Moses for their children and following generations, they developed a system of synagogues. This was a local center where reciting prayers, singing Psalms, and teaching the Law were practiced every Sabbath day. A synagogue was required in every town or village where there were at least ten adult Jewish males. This local center of Jewish life continued long after the Jews returned to Jerusalem and rebuilt the Temple. Over the centuries, scattered across the nations, there were synagogues in almost every city, town, or village, where Jewish families lived.

Early in the Fourth Century B.C. the Greek army, led by Alexander the Great, marched from Greece eastward conquering everything in their path. Alexander's death in 323 B.C., ended the Greek expansion and precipitated the division of the conquered regions among Alexander's generals.

Seleucus controlled Babylon and the northeastern region, which included the defeated empire of the Persians. His unwavering determination to bring the Greek gods and practices to his entire domain galvanized the Greek culture in this area.

Ptolemy I Lagos controlled the southern region, which included Palestine and Egypt. His rule granted the Jews in Jerusalem much liberty and freedom to worship in the rebuilt Temple according to the Law of Moses.

These kingdoms continued until the king of the north, Antiochus IV, called Epiphanes, invaded the southern kingdom late in the Second Century B.C. Antiochus, having conquered Palestine, required the Jews to abandon their worship of Jehovah and their keeping of the Mosaic Law. He set up an image of the Greek gods in the Temple and desecrated the altar by offering swine in the holy place. He met with great opposition by a group, who later became known as the Maccabees. These heroic Jewish leaders defeated the Greeks and, having cleansed the Temple, restored the worship of Jehovah. Thus, was established a yearly winter festival called the Feast of Dedication, commemorating the cleansing of the Temple (Jn. 10:22). The primary change in Jewish government by these new rulers from the Maccabean family (Hasmonean Dynasty) was that they became both civil rulers and high priests, a practice they determined to continue until the coming of the Messiah. It was during this era that two powerful sects of Judaism emerged, called the Pharisees and the Sadducees.

The plan of the Hasmonean rulers was abruptly halted by the arrival of the Roman General Pompey in 63 B.C. The Jews were now under the dominion of Rome, and the Roman rulers appointed whomever they chose to govern Judea. They chose Herod the Great, a brilliant, yet insane Iduemean as the "king of the Jews". Under Herod, the Jews continued to be self-governing by a 70-member council called the Sanhedrin and the High Priest who was usually appointed by the Roman ruler. Herod attempted to win the favor of the Jews by building them a new and grand Temple. This project, that began in 20 B.C. continued long after Herod's death and was not fully completed until A.D. 64.

These significant events prepared the world for the coming of Christ. The conquest of the Greeks brought the world the Greek language. While every region maintained its own native language, the Greek language became a common language of all people breaking down the barriers of communication.

The Jewish synagogues were established throughout Israel and the world. These became a focal point for evangelism. The first Christian converts were Jews, and the proclamation of the gospel began in the Jewish synagogue in almost every city. As Paul and his missionary team traveled the world, they usually began their ministry in the synagogue.

The Romans gave the empire a season of peace and stability, the advancement of education by a public-school system created a literate society, and an advanced network of roads and postal service made travel and correspondence easier throughout the empire.

For the first time in human history, these factors created a positive environment for all peoples of the known world to hear and receive the gospel of Jesus Christ.

The Reason the Temple in Jerusalem Was Known as Herod's Temple

King Herod was a brilliant builder, and he built many cities in honor of important people. He built the city of Caesarea in honor of Caesar and rebuilt the city of Samaria naming it Sebaste in honor of Augustus. Many of the architectural wonders found in Masada and Athens along with various temples, hippodromes, and amphitheaters were the work of this evil genius. The most outstanding achievement of King Herod was the building of the Temple in Jerusalem. His purpose for many of the elaborate building projects was to help him find favor with the people, for Herod needed much favor with those he ruled over. As "king of the Jews" he struggled to gain support from the Jewish leadership, and building a temple to rival Solomon's might go a long way in establishing Jewish favor. Although a temple stood on Jerusalem's Temple Mount, it was very much inferior in both size and splendor to the Temple Solomon constructed.

Herod convinced the Jewish leadership of his desire to build them a Temple, but they were skeptical of his intentions even though Herod himself was a proselyte to Judaism.

In the days of the Hasmonean dynasty, the Maccabees defeated the Iduemeans and forcibly required their conversion to Judaism. Herod was a product of his families past conversion, which was helpful to him in governing the region as "king of the Jews". His loyalty to Rome brought much criticism from his Jewish subjects, and they were concerned that he may destroy their Temple and not rebuild as he promised. Consequently, Herod trained the Jews as masons and workman to assemble the Temple stones he had cut for the project without defiling the Holy Place. This architectural wonder began by Herod creating a foundation around the perimeter of the Temple Mount and filling it with earth to create an additional 26 acres of property for the buildings. Although this grand project began in 20 B.C., it was not completed until A.D. 64, long after Herod's death, but the building was much grander than even Solomon's Temple. Massive plates of gold surrounded the entry gate walls with golden clusters of grapes as tall as a man hung from the walls. At the time of Jesus' ministry, the Temple had been under construction for 46 years (Jn. 2:20), and new construction was being added regularly so that the disciples were excited to show Jesus the new buildings on his last visit to Jerusalem (Mt. 24:1).

Jesus predicted the destruction of the Temple within one generation (Lk. 21:5,6,32). This was fulfilled 40 years later when the Romans marched on the city of Jerusalem, destroying the city and the Temple.

Jewish Influence and Government

The people of the Jewish nation were under the dominion of Rome; therefore, they were required to pay taxes and tribute to Caesar and the various Roman rulers. These taxes and tolls were collected by the Publicans who were Jews employed by the Roman government. This common practice of conquered people paying taxes through those hired from their own nation was believed to lessen the hostility they might feel toward their captures. These publicans were hated by the Jewish community and were treated with contempt because they were viewed as traitors to Israel and because they collected more than the Romans required in order to fill their own pockets. Publicans were usually wealthy, yet despised.

The Jews were large in number and controlled a great deal of wealth. They were allowed to govern themselves under the oversight of the local Roman ruler. The primary ruling body of the Jews was known as the Sanhedrin (meaning to "sit together"). This was a 70-member council made up of both Pharisees and Sadducees under the leadership of the High Priest. This "high court" was the decision-making council and was located in Jerusalem.

Judaism was comprised of many religious sects each with their own particular belief system and function. The most familiar of these sects was the Pharisees.

After the Jews had returned from exile in Babylon in the fifth century B.C., a group of non-priests, made up of scribes and lawyers, gained recognition as an authority to interpret the Law of Moses. These Pharisees (the name taken from the Hebrew word Pharash meaning "set apart") gained popularity among the people. Among the many things taught by this group was that the Davidic Kingdom would be reestablished when the Messiah was revealed. They also taught many of the oral traditions handed down by the Rabbis. Jesus condemned these oral traditions and all who taught them (Mk. 7:13). The Pharisees were a political party who were always in conflict with the Sadducees, another of these Jewish sects. The Pharisees gained much power when the Roman general Pompey marched into Palestine and favored the Pharisees above the Sadducees. Later, when King Herod came to power, he executed 45 members of the Sadducees who were all members of the Sanhedrin (the governing body of the Jews) and had opposed him. There were about 6,000 Pharisees in Jesus' day who were the objects of his condemnation (Mt. 23).

Another of the primary sects of the Jewish leadership was the Sadducees. Although not as popular as the Pharisees, this sect ruled the Temple markets and controlled a considerable amount of wealth generated at the Temple. These were the modernists who believed only in the written word, and yet they denied the existence of spirits and any future resurrection.

The Sadducees were named from Sadok, a pupil of Antigonus Sodraeus, who was president of the Sanhedrin and lived in the third century B.C. Sodraeus taught the "duty of serving God disinterestedly without hope of reward or fear of punishment." Sadok, believed that there was no future state of rewards or punishments and no resurrection and that the soul of man perishes with his body at death. (The Life and Times of Jesus the Messiah, Alfred Edersheim, Book 3, Chapter 2, page 219).

The Herodians were a political party of Sadducees who favored the Herods. Herod the Great died shortly after the birth of Jesus, but Herod's children and grandchildren continued rule in the region. Aristobulus, Herodias, Agrippa I, Agrippa II were just a few of the descendants of Herod the Great. The Herodians courted the favor of these rulers in an attempt to destroy Jesus (Mk. 3:6).

Chapter 4

The Boyhood of Jesus

The only Biblical account of Jesus during his early years is recorded in Luke's gospel when Jesus was twelve years of age (Lk. 2:41-52). Joseph and Mary attended the Passover Feast in Jerusalem every year. A caravan from Nazareth would travel together the 60 miles to Jerusalem carrying friends, neighbors and family members. After the Passover the caravan would return to Nazareth. You can imagine the interaction of family members and close friends on this joyful occasion --the children playing together along the way as the adults discussed the latest news and events they heard about while attending the weeklong celebration. Joseph and Mary did not know Jesus had not joined the caravan but had remained in the city of Jerusalem. At the conclusion of the first day's travel, they began looking for Jesus among their family members and acquaintances as they prepared their campsite. When they did not find Jesus, they arose early the next morning and anxiously hurried back to Jerusalem to find their son. Luke records that they searched for him for three days before finding him in the Temple.

Where did these frantic parents search for their son? Most likely they would have looked in all of the usual places you would expect to find a twelve-year old boy. Having exhausted the search of the ball fields, parks, and fishing holes, they returned to the Temple, and there they saw Jesus sitting among the doctors, scribes, rabbis and teachers, both asking questions and giving answers. Even at this young age, Jesus impressed this elite group of scholars, for they were "astonished at his understanding and answers." Mary's rebuke of Jesus for not telling them he was staying behind was countered with Jesus' expectation that they would understand his need "to be about his Father's business." Although they did not understand, we see that Jesus understood who his Father was and desired to please him. Jesus returned to Nazareth with Joseph and Mary and obeyed them as he "increased in wisdom and stature, and in favor with God and man" (Lk 2:52).

Except for this one account of Jesus, nothing is written about him from age twelve to age 30. These are known as the silent years. There are other accounts of the childhood of Jesus in the apocrypha books that speak of him creating a bird from clay and making it come alive and raising a playmate from the dead after a serious fall, but none of these are accurate for John records the first miracle of Jesus was turning the water to wine at the wedding feast in Cana.

There are only glimpses into the home life of Jesus during these silent years. One of the things we do know is that Jesus was part of a blended family with a stepfather and half brothers and sisters. There were many potential struggles of this blended family. His brothers did not believe he was the Christ until after his resurrection (Jn. 7:5). His father (a beloved family member) died, and as patriarch of the family, Jesus consequently took on the responsibility of caring for his mother as well as his brothers and sisters. He also had to run the family business. These stresses mirror many of the stresses of life we all face in some form or another. Jesus was truly "touched" with our weaknesses, having experienced everything as we do, and yet he overcame all of the opposition as an example for us.

Jesus was also aware of who his real Father was and his mission as the Savior of the world. His understanding that he must "be about [his] Father's business" (Lk. 2:49) was seen at the Temple when he was a child. From that time until his thirtieth birthday Jesus read and studied the scriptures, learning of his purpose and mission as the prophets described it.

Can you imagine Jesus reading Isaiah 61:1-3 to discover the anointing he would receive? Reading in Isaiah 53:3, he understood that he would be "despised and rejected of men." As he read Psalms 22:16, he would see the form of death he would experience in the words, "they pierced my hands and my feet." As Jesus read from the prophet Daniel, he would discover that he was the one who would "finish the transgression, and …make an end of sins, and …make reconciliation for iniquity, and …bring in everlasting righteousness" (Dan. 9:24). From reading the scriptures, Jesus knew of his foretold birth in Bethlehem (Mic. 5:2), the resurrection he would experience (Ps. 16:10), and his ascension into heaven (Ps. 68:18; Dan. 7:13,14). He could see in the written word of God his purpose and destiny.

Chapter 5

The Judean Ministry – The Year of Obscurity

It is no coincidence that Jesus left Nazareth to begin conducting his Father's business as the Messiah (the Anointed One) at the age of thirty years. As we see in Matthew's Gospel (Mt. 5:17), Jesus clearly states that he "came not to destroy the law, or the prophets… but to fulfill" them. Under the Law of Moses, there were age requirements for the Levites to minister in the Tabernacle. The priests, who were also Levites, could not begin their appointed ministry until thirty years of age (Num. 4:43-47). Jesus was to be the eternal High Priest after the order of Melchisedec, so it was at the age of thirty that Jesus left the town of Nazareth and headed south through the Jordan valley to where John the Baptist was baptizing.

There is no indication in scripture that John and Jesus had ever met before. Both John's mother Elisabeth and Mary, the mother of Jesus, spent 3 months together prior to the birth of John. Each had a prophetic word about the mission of their yet unborn sons. John was to carry the message that the Messiah was coming, and he had been sent as a forerunner to turn the hearts of the people back to God in preparation for Jesus' ministry. John said, "And I knew him not: but he that sent me to baptize with water, the same said unto me, Upon whom you [shall] see the Spirit descending, and remaining on him, the same is he which [baptizes] with the Holy [Spirit]. And I saw, and bare record that this is the Son of God" (Jn. 1:33,34).

At the Jordan River near Jericho, John had been baptizing multitudes of people who had responded to his message. When Jesus arrived at the Jordan, he requested John to baptize him in the river. John, knowing by the Spirit that this one who stood before him was the Son of God, said to Jesus, "I have need to be baptized of thee, and comest thou to me?" (Mt. 3:14) or in more updated language, "I need you to baptize me and you want me to baptize you?" John's message to the multitudes was that the Messiah would come, and when he came, he will baptize with the Spirit of God, so when Jesus stood before him, John was hoping to be baptized in the Spirit. However, Jesus needed to be baptized by John for two reasons. First, Jesus would receive John's testimony that Jesus was the Messiah (Jn. 1:29). Second, it was as Jesus was baptized in water that the Spirit of God descended upon him and he became the Christ, "the Anointed One" (Mt. 3:16). It was then that God the Father spoke from heaven, bearing witness that Jesus was the Son of God (Mt. 3:17). Jesus received the testimony of both man and God and was anointed and empowered by the Holy Spirit.

Jesus never worked any miracles until he received the anointing of the Holy Spirit. It was not because he was the Son of God that he performed such notable miracles, but because he was empowered by the Holy Spirit (Acts 10:38). Jesus said to his disciples, "Verily, verily

I say unto you, He that believes on me, the works that I do shall he do also; and greater works than these shall he do; because I go unto the Father" (Jn. 14:12). The reason it was necessary for Jesus to go to the Father was to send the Holy Spirit (the Comforter) to empower those who believe (Jn. 16:7). It was by the empowering of the Holy Spirit that believers could fulfill the great commission of preaching, healing, teaching all nations, and doing miracles (Mt. 28:18-20; Lk. 24:49; Mk. 16:15-18; Acts 1:8).

Temptation in the Wilderness

After Jesus was empowered by the Holy Spirit, he was led into the wilderness to be tempted by the devil. East of the Jordan River, across from the city of Jericho, lay the Perean wilderness. There, Jesus fasted for 40 days. At the end of this time, the devil came to him with three specific temptations. John tells us that there are only three temptations that mankind faces, "For all that is in the world, the lust of the flesh, and the lust of the eyes, and the pride of life, is not of the Father, but is of the world" (1 Jn. 2:16). The Book of Hebrews tells us that Jesus was tempted in every area as we are, yet he did not sin (4:15). It was necessary for Jesus to overcome all temptation to sin. He was to be the perfect sacrifice without blemish (the Lamb of God that takes away the sin of the world), and his victory was not only for himself but also for all mankind. He was living a perfect, holy, and sinless life in order to give us his righteousness (Rom. 5:17).

The first temptation Jesus faced was concerning the lust of the flesh. He had not eaten for 40 days, and he became hungry. Physiologically, a person fasting for an extended period of time loses the feeling of hunger, but once hunger returns it is expedient to eat because starvation has begun. At his weakest moment, Jesus was faced with this thought, "If you be the Son of God, command this stone that it be made bread" (Lk. 4:3). Many believe that the devil appeared to Jesus during this time of temptation and that may be so, but I believe that these temptations were subtler than that. If Jesus was tempted in every way as we are, then I believe the devil did not visibly appear but came to Jesus as a thought. After all, Jesus was the Son of God, and he had a legitimate need. He could have turned stone into bread, but Jesus never did anything as the Son of God, but as the son of man, anointed by the Holy Spirit, and only in obedience to the voice of God (Jn. 5:19,30; 6:38). Jesus recognized that the origin of that thought was founded in the lust of the flesh, and he rebuked it, saying, "It is written, That man shall not live by bread alone, but by every word of God" (Lk. 4:4).

The second temptation was dealing with the lust of the eyes. Luke's account says the devil took Jesus to a high mountain and showed him all the kingdoms of the world in a moment of time. Some translations say "at one time" or "in the twinkling of an eye". Again, we know there is no physical location where we can see all the kingdoms of the world at once, but in our minds, we can go anywhere without restriction or limitation. It seems that this temptation was not as subtle as the first, for the devil spoke to Jesus, offering him all the kingdoms of the world and the glory of possessing them. The devil also declared that the kingdoms of the world had been delivered to him. Jesus did not argue with that statement because, truly, Adam had delivered the authority God had given to him over the kingdoms of the world to the tempter. We know the kingdom of God is not of this world and neither are those believers who are a part of God's kingdom. We also know that there will come a time when the kingdoms of the world shall become the kingdoms of the Lord (Rev. 11:15). This temptation was real. Satan had promised Jesus the glory and greatness of all that the world's kingdoms could offer if only Jesus would worship him. Jesus would not be deceived and rebuked Satan, declaring the command of God's word, "Thou shalt worship the Lord thy God, and him only shall you serve" (Lk. 4:5-8).

The last temptation was an appeal to the pride of life. Once again the devil had to physically transport Jesus to the Temple in the city of Jerusalem or just suggest to his mind this thought, "Why not go to the Temple and stand on the highest place at the pinnacle where everyone in the city can see you and jump off knowing that the scripture says God has given his angels a charge of keeping you safe from even stubbing your toe against a stone; and then just before you hit the ground, the angels will surround you and gently set you down, and everyone in Jerusalem will see who you are" (my paraphrase). This time, Satan was using scripture to try and validate this idea, but Jesus, knowing the source of this thought, again quoted the scriptures saying, "It is said, you shall not tempt the Lord your God" (Lk. 4:9-12). After this statement, the devil ended all the temptations and departed from Jesus for a season.

Having overcome every temptation, Jesus left the wilderness and returned to where John the Baptist was baptizing at the Jordan River. John acknowledged Jesus as the Lamb of God who takes away the sin of the world. The next day Jesus again came to John the Baptist who again said to the crowd around him, "Behold the Lamb of God" (Jn. 1:29, 35,36). This time, two of John's disciples heard him refer to Jesus as the Lamb of God, and they followed Jesus. Jesus invited them to stay with him for that day. We know that one of these two men was Andrew who was Simon Peter's brother. Andrew found Peter and brought him to Jesus. Then the next day Jesus called Philip, and Philip in turn found his friend Nathanael and brought him to Jesus. By the end of the second day, after Jesus returned from the wilderness, he had Andrew, Peter, Philip, Nathanael and one other of the original two who is not named. Scholars suppose that the other disciple was John who never recognizes himself by name in his gospel. Very probably John and his brother James who were part of Jesus' inner circle were also present. This can be assumed because, when Peter stood among the 120 (Acts 1), he gave the requirements for the one who was to replace Judas the betrayer. Peter suggested that whoever was selected should have "companied with us all the time that the Lord Jesus went in and out among us, beginning from the baptism of John, unto the same day that he was taken up from us…" (Acts 1:21,22). Although Jesus did not choose, of his many disciples, the twelve whom he named apostles until his second year of ministry (Lk. 6:13), Peter implies that the replacement for Judas (who betrayed Jesus) should have been with Jesus when he was baptized by John the Baptist.

THE FIRST MIRACLE – WATER TO WINE

The third day after returning from the wilderness Jesus, along with his first six disciples, leave the Jordan River in Judea and travel north, through the Jordan Valley into Galilee. There, Jesus enters the city of Cana and attends a marriage with his disciples. Although the bride and groom are not identified, we can presume that the wedding involved one of Jesus' brothers because his mother Mary is obviously in charge of the servants.

We know that Jesus had four half-brothers (children born to Joseph and Mary) and at least two half-sisters. Their names are recorded in the Gospel of Mark (Mk. 6:3) James, Joses, Juda, and Simon and his sisters, although unnamed, are in the plural form. A casual reading of John Chapter 2 reveals the events that surround this first miracle performed by Jesus, but if we take a closer look, we can discover so much more.

First of all, we need to know some things about Jewish weddings and customs. One example is found in Jacob's marriage to Laban's daughter (Gen. 29). There we see that Jacob had left his father's house to escape Esau's wrath and journeyed to his uncle Laban's house. He was warmly received by Laban and his family and soon went to work for Laban. In time Jacob fell in love with Rachel, Laban's youngest daughter and because he had no means to pay a dowry to Laban in order to marry Rachel, Jacob and Laban made an agreement that Jacob would work for Laban for seven years to pay the dowry. At the end of the time, Jacob went to Laban and demanded Rachel as his wife. Laban agreed, and the seven-day marriage feast began. We know the story of Laban's deceit as he brought his oldest daughter Leah to Jacob instead. Because Leah was heavily veiled, Jacob did not discover until the morning that she was his wife, not Rachel. Jacob's anger against Laban was met with his uncle's explanation of their custom to marry the oldest daughter first. Laban now gave Jacob an option of also receiving Rachel as his wife after he fulfilled the seven-day marriage feast for Leah if he would work for another seven years. Jacob agreed to the new arrangement.

This story gives us a biblical account of the marriage feast lasting seven days. It is also well documented in Jewish social life that this was still the custom in Jesus' day; however, a week-long wedding feast was more typical for the wealthy who could afford the luxury of hosting a large crowd for that length of time. This brings us to some facts about Jesus and his family that are not often talked about.

The last account of Joseph, Mary's husband, was when Jesus was twelve years old (Lk. 2:41-52). We know Joseph was known as the Carpenter in Nazareth. Since Joseph is described as a good and righteous man, it is not likely that he deserted his family, but must have died prior to Jesus' 30th birthday. In Jewish families, when the husband/father dies, the oldest son assumes the position as the new patriarch of the family. He receives a much larger inheritance than the other siblings because he becomes responsible for his mother and his brothers and sisters. In New Testament times, it was also typical for the sons to follow their father in the family business. We know Jesus became known as the Carpenter, in place of his father (Mt. 13:55). We have no idea how long Jesus filled this position after Joseph died, but here is what we do know. The scriptures promise that to those who "hearken diligently unto the voice of the Lord [their] God, to observe and to do all his commandments ….all these blessings shall come on [them], and overtake [them]…" (Deut. 28:1,2). Among the many promised blessings to those who listen diligently to the voice of God and obey it are the filling up of their storehouses and blessing all they set their hand to do, making them prosperous, blessing their businesses and increasing them in every good thing and much more as described in Deuteronomy 28. If there was ever anyone who perfectly fulfilled the commandments of God, it was Jesus. I believe he must have been the most successful and prosperous carpenter who ever lived. It is also worth knowing that a carpenter in Jesus' day was more like a general contractor today. One who built using different types of materials, not just wood. The conditions at the wedding feast revealed the prosperity of this family. There were servants to carry out Mary's commands, and there was the "governor of the feast" (the wedding planner) who oversaw the events of the seven-day feast.

Here is another example of Jesus being tempted in every way like we are. He experienced the death of a loved one and was willing to leave the security and benefits of a thriving business to pursue the will of God his Father. His brothers did not understand Jesus' leaving the responsibilities as head of the family. For this reason, they did not believe on him and agreed that Jesus was "beside himself," meaning out of his mind (Mk. 3:21).

Sometime after arriving at the wedding feast, Jesus was approached by his mother, who informed him that they had run out of wine. As the head of the family, it would have been Jesus' responsibility to see that more wine was purchased; however, Jesus responded to his mother from a different position. He was now fulfilling the will of his Heavenly Father; his time had come when he "must be about his Father's business," even at the cost of forsaking his earthly family. But Mary knew Jesus would take care of the problem. She was not expecting a miraculous work, for Jesus had never before performed a miracle; she only knew he would make the necessary arrangements to meet the need, so she informed the servants to do whatever he told them. Six stone water pots stood in the adjoining room that would hold about nine gallons each. Jesus instructed the servants to fill the pots with water and then draw out a cup of water and deliver it to the wedding planner for his approval. After tasting the water that had become wine sometime during the journey from the next room, the wedding planner called the groom over to question his reason for serving the best wine towards the end of the feast days, saying, "Every man at the beginning does set forth good wine; and when men have well drunk, then that which is worse; but you have kept the good wine until now" (Jn. 2:10). This miracle of turning water into wine was the very first miracle Jesus performed. This miraculous work "[shown] forth his glory;" and "his disciples believed on him" (Jn. 2:11).

MIRACLES REVEAL THE GLORY OF GOD

Many times, in the gospels, we see the results of miraculous works and what those miracles produced in the minds of those who witnessed them. Here at the wedding feast in Cana, turning water into wine caused his disciples to believe in Jesus (Jn. 2:11). They already had the testimony of John the Baptist, but now this miracle revealed the glory of God and confirmed to the disciples that Jesus was the Messiah.

After John the Baptist was arrested, he sent his disciples to Jesus with this question: "Are you he that should come, or do we look for another?" (Mt. 11:3). Jesus did not directly answer John's question, but instead told his disciples to return to John and tell him what they had seen, "the blind receive their sight, and the lame walk, the lepers are cleansed, and the deaf hear, the dead are raised up, and the poor have the gospel preached to them" (Mt. 11:5). It was the witness of these miracles that would confirm to John that Jesus was the one that John himself had preached about.

Jesus had borrowed Peter's boat to teach from as the crowds of people gathered on the shoreline of the Sea of Galilee. When Jesus ended his teaching, he turned to Peter and told him to take the boat out into the deeper water and let down the nets, and they would catch fish. Peter was a little slow to respond to Jesus, saying that they had already fished all night and did not catch anything, but reluctantly he obeyed the instructions of Jesus. After letting down the nets, they caught many fish, so many in fact, that both of the boats were almost sinking under the weight of the haul of fish. When Peter saw what had happened, he fell down at Jesus' feet and said, "Depart from me, for I am a sinful man, O Lord" (Lk. 5:8). Peter, and all of the disciples who were present were astonished at the number of fish that were taken and recognized it as a miraculous work.

Jesus proclaimed that he cast out demons by the Spirit of God and thus manifested, God's kingdom (Mt. 12:28). These miracles revealed the power of God working through Jesus and showed his authority as Lord over the Sabbath, as well as his right to forgive sins (Mk. 2:28; Lk. 5:24).

Jesus in Capernaum and Jerusalem

Leaving Cana of Galilee, Jesus traveled to the city of Capernaum. His disciples, his brothers, and his mother went with him from the wedding feast. It was springtime, and the Feast of Passover was soon to begin in Jerusalem. Jesus left Capernaum with his disciples and made the nearly sixty-mile trip to Jerusalem. Upon his arrival, he entered the Temple and there found many oxen and sheep and cages filled with doves next to the moneychangers in the outer court. Jesus' anger moved him to make a whip and drive the animals out of the Temple court while overturning the tables of the moneychangers. He also commanded the cages of doves to be removed, saying, "make not my Father's house an house of merchandise" (Jn. 2:13-16).

What a scene it must have been as the Temple gates were opened and these valuable animals are driven into the street while the gold and silver coins were rolling on the ground and the moneychangers were chasing their scattering merchandise. The selling of sacrificial animals at the Temple was a very lucrative business. Those worshippers making the pilgrimage to Jerusalem for the feast days were not allowed to purchase animals of sacrifice with Roman currency. They first had to exchange Roman currency for Temple currency for a hefty fee. Then, with the Temple currency, they could purchase the priest approved animals for sacrifice. The inflated currency fees and high prices required for purchasing the animals were unjust, causing Jesus to call these Temple merchants, "a den of thieves" (Mt. 21:13).

The outer court of the Temple was the court of prayer. This is where the people would gather for the morning and evening sacrifices. Worshippers were praying in the outer court while the officiating priest would take a hot coal from off the brazen altar and carry it into the Holy Place before the veil and sprinkle incenses on it, creating a fragrant smoke that would filter beyond the veil into the Most Holy Place before the presence of God. The smoke of the incense represented the prayers of the worshippers. This place of prayer was not being used for prayer, but for the merchandising of the Temple rulers. The people were not only being robbed financially, but the benefits of prayer were lost. Once the outer court had been purged by Jesus, the people came for prayer, and "the blind and the lame came to him in the temple, and he healed them" (Mt. 21:14).

Cleansing the Temple was both the first and last things Jesus did in Jerusalem during his season of ministry. John's account shows us Jesus cleansing the Temple at the first Feast of Passover after his anointing and baptism (Jn. 2:13). Matthew's account shows Jesus cleansing the Temple just days prior to his crucifixion on the Feast of Passover (Mt. 21:12). This was not the result of an errant timeline of events, but of two separate occasions when Jesus cleansed the Temple. He was determined to fulfill the purpose of God the Father in making the Temple a house of prayer (Isa. 56:7; Mt. 21:13).

The Jewish leaders burned with anger against Jesus for upsetting their profiteering. They quickly appeared on the scene and demanded a sign of his authority to do what he had done. Jesus responded to them by saying, "Destroy this temple, and in three days I will raise it up" (Jn. 2:19). They understood him to mean the physical temple that had been under construction for forty-six years, but Jesus was referring to the sign of his resurrection from the dead after three days. It was only after his resurrection that his disciples understood his words (Jn. 2:22).

After this first conflict with the Jewish leaders in Jerusalem, Jesus stayed in the city and performed many miracles, which caused many to believe that he was indeed the Christ (Jn. 2:23, 3:2, 4:45).

Nicodemus Searching for the Truth

While Jesus was still in Jerusalem one of the Pharisees who was also a member of the ruling council known as the Sanhedrin came to him. His name was Nicodemus. Under the cover of night, he came quietly calling Jesus "Rabbi" and confessing, "We know that you are a teacher come from God: for no man can do these miracles that you do, except God be with him" (Jn. 3:2). Apparently, Nicodemus revealed a discussion the council must have had, acknowledging that Jesus had come from God. Later on, it is revealed that many of the chief rulers believed on Jesus, "but because of the Pharisees they did not confess him, lest they should be put out of the synagogue: For they loved the praise of men more than the praise of God" (Jn. 12:42,43).

Nicodemus had a sincere desire for the truth, a desire which Jesus readily perceived. Instead of waiting for Nicodemus to ask him a question, Jesus gave him the answer to the question he never got to ask, saying, "Truly, truly, I say unto you, except a man be born again he cannot see the kingdom of God" (Jn. 3:3). Nicodemus' reply brought further explanation by Jesus. Being birthed was a physiological event to Nicodemus, something that could never be repeated. However, Jesus explained the difference between being born physically and being born spiritually. These births are two separate events from two completely different sources. That which is flesh can only produce flesh, but that which is born of the Spirit is spiritual. Confusion filled Nicodemus, who asked, "How can these things be?" and Jesus replied, "[Are] you a master of Israel and you don't know these things?" Nicodemus had the best education and possessed the highest level of recognition one could achieve, the "ruler of the Jews" and a member of the highest court in Israel, but he was ignorant of spiritual things.

Jesus' next statement must have puzzled Nicodemus even more. He said, "We speak that we do know, and testify that we have seen; and you receive not our witness. If I have told you earthly things, and you believe not, how shall you believe, if I tell you of heavenly things?" (Jn. 3:11,12). There is no indication in this passage of scripture that anyone else was present while Nicodemus and Jesus talked. No servants of the ruler or disciples of Jesus are mentioned. It appears that Nicodemus purposely sought out Jesus privately to keep his inquiry confidential. Who then is the "we" and "our" referred to here?

Jesus often referred to the fact that he and his Father are one. Jesus speaks the words of his Father and does the works of his Father (Jn. 14:10). Jesus is anointed by the Holy Spirit (Lk. 4:18), and it is by the power of the Holy Spirit that every miracle is performed (Acts 10:38). Jesus, therefore, was not only speaking of himself, but he was speaking from the Father and the anointing of the Holy Spirit. He then further revealed the qualities of spiritual things, showing the ruler of the Jews that, while Jesus was standing on the streets of Jerusalem speaking to him, Jesus was also positioned in heaven (Jn. 3:13). Physical birth brings physical limitations, but Jesus was attempting to show Nicodemus the unlimited aspects of spiritual things.

Jesus continued to reveal to Nicodemus his purpose and mission. This portion of scripture concludes without any further response from Nicodemus, but this interview with Jesus must have had a great impact on him. During the Feast of Tabernacles, the Sanhedrin sent officers to arrest Jesus. After hearing Jesus speak, they returned to the council without having arrested him with the excuse that they had never heard any man speak the things they heard Jesus speak. The council deemed the officers "deceived" by Jesus and then asked this question: "Have any of the rulers of the Pharisees believed on him?" (Jn. 7:48). Nicodemus spoke up in defense of Jesus (Jn. 7:50,51). Nicodemus revealed further loyalty to Jesus when he helped Joseph of Arimathaea prepare the body of Jesus for burial and laid him in the tomb on the day of his crucifixion (Jn. 19:38-42). The actions of Nicodemus seem to confirm that he became a believer and disciple of Jesus.

The End of the Judean Ministry

John's is the only gospel to mention the events of the first year of Jesus' ministry beyond his baptism and temptation in the wilderness. Thanks to John's account, we have the call of the first disciples; the marriage feast in Cana; the first cleansing of the Temple; the visit of Nicodemus and the final events of that first year, known as the year of obscurity.

This period of time ended with Jesus and his disciples leaving Jerusalem and traveling twenty miles east to the Jordan River. John the Baptist was still baptizing in the Jordan River when Jesus and his disciples also began baptizing, even though the scriptures mention that Jesus did not personally baptize anyone, but his disciples did. When John's disciples recognized that the crowds of people were no longer coming to John but to Jesus instead, they became jealous for John and informed him of what was taking place not far down river from him. John understood that his mission and purpose was to identify Jesus as the Messiah. John saw himself as the "friend of the bridegroom." The bridegroom was Jesus. John was not the husband of the bride because, unlike Jesus, whose heavenly origin was from above, John's origin was from the earth. John knew that Jesus must increase, and that he [John] must decrease, for Jesus was speaking the "words of God and had the Spirit without measure" (Jn. 3:29-34).

John the Baptist had a clear understanding of who Jesus was and what he had come to do, for he instructed his disciples and all who heard him by saying, "He that believes on the Son has everlasting life: and he that believes not the Son shall not see life; but the wrath of God abides on him" (Jn. 3:36).

Jesus remained at the river until he knew that the Pharisees had heard that he "made and baptized more disciples than John" (Jn. 4:1). This was not a competition between John and Jesus. The multitudes of people and the religious leaders themselves recognized John the Baptist as a prophet of God. The number of those coming to Jesus was evidence to everyone that Jesus was superior to John and confirmed John's own testimony about Jesus. Once Jesus knew these things had been accomplished, he left Judea on his way to Galilee, but he knew that first "he must go through Samaria" (Jn. 4:4).

Jesus Traveling through Samaria

Before we look at the encounter Jesus had with the woman at the well we need to know a few things about Samaria. After King Solomon's death (931 B.C.) the nation of Israel was divided into two nations. Israel was the northern kingdom with a king who ruled from the capital city called Samaria and the southern kingdom known as Judah whose king ruled from the city of Jerusalem. All of the kings of Judah were of the lineage of king David, while none of the kings of Israel were from David's line, but were from different dynasties.

Eventually, the northern kingdom of Israel was defeated by the Assyrians, and the citizens of Israel were forcefully dispersed among the many cities of Assyria. The Assyrian king brought people from other regions to populate the land of Israel who intermarried with the few Israelites that were able to remain in the land. This became a new nation, eventually known as Samaria. The new inhabitants worshipped many pagan gods, but they made a request of the king of Assyria to send a priest of Jehovah to teach them how to worship him because they reasoned he was the god of that region, and if they offered sacrifices to him, he would protect them from the lions that had been attacking them. A priest was sent, and the Samaritans began to worship the God of Israel. The heresy of their worship was not that they recognized Jehovah as God, but that they just added Jehovah to the many different gods they already worshipped.

After Judah (the southern kingdom) was exiled under the Babylonians for 70 years and then allowed to return and rebuild the city of Jerusalem and the Temple, they were threatened by the Samaritans for not allowing them to help in the rebuilding of the Temple. Both Ezra and Nehemiah refused to work with the Samaritans because of their worship of many pagan gods even though they had added Jehovah to their polytheistic list. Upon his arrival from Babylon, Ezra discovered that some of the priests had married Samaritan women, a violation of the Law of Moses. Even the son of the high priest had married the daughter of Sanballat, who was a ruler in Samaria. Ezra gave an ultimatum to the priests to either divorce their Samaritan wives or leave the priesthood. Sanballat offered the disobedient priests an opportunity to serve in his rival temple which he had built on Mt. Gerizim near the city of Syhcar in southern Samaria. This temple near Sychar remained for almost two hundred years until the Maccabeus destroyed it.

It was by the military might of the Maccabean rulers that the surrounding nations became proselytes to Judaism, which included Samaria. Again, the Samaritans worshipped Jehovah, but the orthodox

Jews refused to recognize them, causing great strife and animosity. That is why the "Jews had no dealings with the Samaritans" (Jn. 4:9).

Many of the Jews in Jesus' day refused to travel through Samaria because of their years of conflict, but it is said of Jesus, "he must needs go through Samaria" (Jn. 4:4).

Instead of following the Jordan valley north to Galilee as most orthodox Jews would, Jesus and his disciples traveled west through Samaria until they reached the city of Sychar. It was about noon, and Jesus was tired from the journey and hungry. He and his disciples would have traveled about twenty miles, so when they reached Sychar, they rested at the well that supplied the water for the city.

Jesus sent the disciples away to buy lunch, and while he waited for their return, a woman came to the well to draw water. Jesus approached her and asked that she let him drink some of the water she had drawn. Her response revealed the tension between the Samaritans and the Jews. She said, "How is it that you, being a Jew, ask for a drink of me, a woman of Samaria? For the Jews have no dealings with the Samaritans" (Jn. 4:9). Jesus answered her with an offer to give her "living water" if she would only ask. The woman, not understanding Jesus' response, questioned his ability to give her the only water she knew about, saying, "this is a deep well and you have nothing with which to draw up the water" (Jn. 4:11, my paraphrase) and then she must have considered the possibility that Jesus had a different source of water, for she informed him of the history of the well that once belonged to Jacob. In this way she was defending her lineage stemming from the patriarch Jacob and questioning Jesus' ability to give her water from a source nobler than Jacob's well.

Jesus begins to describe to her a kind of water she had never heard of, saying, "Those who drink the water I give will never be thirsty again. It becomes a fresh, bubbling spring within them, giving them eternal life" (Jn. 4:14 NLT).

Desiring this life-giving water, she said to Jesus, "Sir, give me this water, that I thirst not, neither come here to draw" (Jn. 4:15). The woman, perceiving that this water Jesus offered would somehow release her from the daily chore of drawing water from the well, was immediately challenged to go get her husband and return to Jesus. The woman retorted, "I have no husband." Jesus, having a word of knowledge, told her that she had had five husbands and that the man she is living with now was not her husband.

Obviously feeling uncomfortable that Jesus knows her sinful lifestyle, she acknowledged him as a prophet and then asked him a question regarding the best location to worship God. Her question referenced the rival temple of Sanballat that was built on nearby Mt. Gerizim. She told Jesus, "Our fathers worshipped in this mountain" (Jn. 4:20). Jesus quickly validated the Jerusalem Temple as the location of worship, but revealed that soon true worship would no longer be in a physical location, but in the spirit and in truth (Jn. 4:23). The woman then revealed to Jesus that she was looking for the Messiah who would come and explain all these things.

There are very few times in the gospels where Jesus says plainly, "I am the Messiah (Christ)", but here is one of those times. It was not to the Jewish religious authorities or prominent leaders, but to a Samaritan woman with a blatant sinful lifestyle who would have been rejected and despised by those in her community. She believed Jesus and ran to the city declaring that she had just met the Messiah, shouting, he "told me all things that ever I did: is not this the Christ?" (Jn. 4:29). Those who heard her announcement immediately hurried to the well to see Jesus.

Jesus often sought out the outcasts. He did not follow the social rules of the day, for it would have been improper for a man to engage a woman in conversation. His disciples, having accomplished their mission, returned to Jesus with lunch while he was still conversing with the woman, and they "marveled that he talked with her" (Jn.

4:27). Socially unacceptable and contrary to the traditions of men, Jesus sought out the broken and outcast of society to bring them salvation.

The disciples brought Jesus the food they had purchased in the village but were met with Jesus' reply, "I have food to eat you know not of" (Jn. 4:32). After they enquired among themselves about who had already brought him food, Jesus reminded them of his mission, saying, "my [food] is to do the will of him that sent me and to finish his work" (Jn. 4:34). His reference may have been to the temptation in the wilderness when he was challenged to turn the stone into bread, but instead declared "man shall not live by bread alone but by every word that proceeds out of the mouth of God" (Mt. 4:4).

The people, hearing the testimony of the woman, came from the city to the well where Jesus was conversing with his disciples. For two days, he remained in the city, teaching the word of God and showing them that he was the Messiah they had been waiting for. The first successful gospel crusade was among a people hated by the religious, despised by the nation, but hungry for the truth. Jesus did not go through Samaria because it was easy or because it was a desired destination on his ministry itinerary, but because he heard the voice of his Father who had sent him to seek and to save that which was lost.

Chapter 6

The Beginning of Jesus' Galilean Ministry

For the next eighteen months, Jesus focused his ministry efforts in the land of Galilee. Galilee is in the northern region of Israel adjacent to the Sea of Galilee. This was a popular and beautiful region of Israel with much commerce where intersecting trade routes brought travelers from many countries. This northern region includes the town of Nazareth where Jesus grew up, Cana where the first miracle was performed at the wedding, and the cities of Chorazin, Bethsaida, and Capernaum that were built on the shores of the Sea of Galilee. This body of water is a fresh water lake that is 700 feet below sea level. The east side of the lake has steep cliffs while the north side of the lake, where the source of its water is supplied from converging streams and underground springs, is more gradually sloped down to the water's edge. Here many notable cities are built, including Capernaum, which houses the seat of the Roman tax collector and military post. The lake itself is approximately 13 miles long and 8 miles wide and provides much industry by commercial fishing.

Having finished his assignment in Samaria, Jesus traveled north to Cana, a city of Galilee. Here he began what is known as his year of popularity. In this region, Jesus performed most of the miracles described in the gospels.

When Jesus arrived in Cana, a nobleman whose son was sick and dying in Capernaum (a city about 20 miles away) met him. This man was an officer in the court of Herod Antipas who was the Tetrarch of Galilee. He had heard of the miracles Jesus had performed at the feast in Jerusalem, for many of the Galileans attended the feast, so when his child became ill, he sought the whereabouts of Jesus. Hearing that Jesus had left Judea and returned to Galilee, he traveled to Cana where he found Jesus and urgently implored him to come to Capernaum and heal his son (Jn. 4:47). "Except you see signs and wonders, you will not believe" (Jn. 4:48) was Jesus' response to the desperate father. The man answered Jesus with great respect, calling him "Sir" which corresponds to one who is supreme in authority, "come down before my child dies" (Jn. 4:49 NIV). This man's acknowledgment of his need for Jesus and his recognition of the absolute authority Jesus carried solicited Jesus response saying, "Go your way; your son lives" (Jn. 4:50). The next day as the nobleman returned to his home, his servants met him with the good news that his son had recovered. Hearing that his fever broke at the same time Jesus said to him, "your son lives," he and his family believed on Jesus.

John tells us in his gospel that this was the second miracle Jesus performed when he came out of Judea into Galilee. The first miracle was turning water into wine at the wedding in this same town nearly a year earlier.

From Cana, Jesus traveled to Capernaum and recalled some of his disciples who had returned to their fishing business. The timeline that would explain when Peter, Andrew, James, and John left Jesus for the shores of Galilee is unknown. At least some disciples, although they are not mentioned by name, were with Jesus in Samaria when he met the woman at the well. We often hear that Jesus had twelve disciples that lived with him day and night for a period of three and a half years, but the reality is that some were not even called to be with him until his second year of ministry. It was in Galilee that he chose twelve from his many disciples to be apostles.

When Jesus entered Capernaum, he went down to the water's edge of the Sea of Galilee where he found Peter and Andrew casting their nets into the sea. He then called them to leave their nets, saying that he would make them "fishers of men" (Mk. 1:17). A little further up the shoreline, he saw James and John, the sons of Zebedee, who were in the boat mending their nets. Jesus called them to once again go with him. They left their father and the servants and rejoined him as he walked into the city.

On the next Sabbath day, Jesus entered the synagogue in Capernaum. His teaching to those in attendance was met with awe and astonishment, for he "taught them as one that had authority, and not as the scribes" (Mk 1:22). Suddenly, a demon possessed man cried out in the synagogue, denouncing Jesus by asking him if he had "come to destroy them?," but also acknowledging that Jesus was the "Holy One of God" (Mk. 1:24). Jesus responded by commanding the unclean spirit to leave the man, who was instantly delivered. This demonstration of authority and power caused the people to be amazed that "even the unclean spirits obey[ed] him" (Mk. 1:27). Jesus became instantly famous as news of this miraculous work quickly spread among the people of Galilee.

Leaving the synagogue with his disciples, he came to Peter and Andrew's house with James and John. Jesus was informed that Peter's mother-in-law was suffering with a fever. He came to her, took her by the hand, and lifted her up. The fever left her, and she began to minister to them. Although there are no details mentioned here, I imagine that she prepared a meal for Jesus, James, John, Andrew, and Simon Peter, and her daughter, Peter's wife. They all probably spent the afternoon resting until the sun went down, and then the Sabbath was over, and suddenly there was a crowd of people at the door of Peter's house. The authority of Jesus' teaching and the demonstration of his power to deliver the demoniac at the synagogue caused nearly the whole city to bring their family members and loved one's who were sick or demon possessed for Jesus to heal them. They waited until the Sabbath was over (sunset) to seek Jesus so as not to violate the Sabbath day and anger the religious leaders. A crowd that large must have required Jesus to minister until late in the night as he "healed many that were sick of different diseases and cast out many demons" (Mk. 1:34). Early the next morning, before sunup, Jesus left Peter's house and went to a place where he could be alone and pray. Soon, Peter and those who were with him found Jesus. They had been looking for him because the crowds had again returned to Peter's house searching for Jesus. There is no mention of Jesus returning to the house at this time, but he invited Simon Peter, Andrew, James, and John to go with him as he, "preached in their synagogues throughout all Galilee" (Mk. 1:38,39).

Choosing the Twelve

The timeline of events regarding Jesus' Galilean ministry are not absolutely certain. The Sermon on the Mount, healing the leper, and his visit to Nazareth may not follow the chronological order in which these events actually happened. However, we know that it was during his second year of ministry that Jesus called twelve of his disciples to be apostles. These apostles would be closest to him and share in his ministry. Among the twelve would be three who would occupy a place of privilege where the others were not permitted.

The twelve tribes of Israel have a very definitive list, but those who would be known as the twelve apostles of the Lamb (Rev. 21:14) are less certain. Judas, the betrayer was replaced by Matthias (Acts 1:26), and yet Saul, who became Paul the apostle, was called "one born out of due time" (1 Cor. 15:8,9). There are many apostles mentioned by name in the Epistles, but those Jesus initially called as apostles are listed in Matthew 10:2, Mark 3:13, Luke 6:13. They are listed in the gospels by these names:

Simon Peter and his brother **Andrew** – Mt. 4:18-20, Mt. 10:2, Mk. 3:16-18, Lk. 6:13,14, Jn. 1:35-42

James and his brother **John**, sons of Zebedee – Mt. 4:21,22, Mt. 10:2, Mk. 3:17, Lk. 6:14

Nathanael also called Bartholomew and **Philip** – Mt. 10:3, Mk. 3:18, Lk. 6:14, Jn. 1:43-51.

Matthew also called Levi, possibly the brother of **James** the son of Alphaeus – Mt. 9:9, 10:3, Mk.2:14, Mk. 3:18, Lk. 6:15.

Thomas, Thaddaeus, also called Lebbaeus or Judas the son of James – Mt. 10:3, Mk. 3:18, Lk. 6:16.

Simon the Zealot, also called the Canaanite – Mt. 10:4, Mk. 3:18, Lk. 6:15 (the word is actually Kananite, a Syro-Chaldeic or Aramaic word for Zealot)

Judas Iscariot – Mt. 10:4, Mk. 3:19, Lk. 6:16.

We know that Simon Peter, Andrew, Nathanael, and Philip had followed Jesus from the baptism of John the Baptist at the very beginning of Jesus' ministry (Jn. 1:35-42). There was another disciple of John the Baptist that followed Jesus who was not named (Jn. 1:37). This may have been John, who in his gospel never mentions himself by name. We also know that Jesus did not call Matthew, who was called Levi, until his Galilean or second year of ministry (Mt. 9:9, Mk. 2:14).

Among these twelve, it is very possible that there were three sets of brothers. Simon Peter and Andrew were brothers, and James and John were also brothers. Matthew or Levi is known as the son of Alphaeus and so is James. These too were possibly brothers.

Another possible family relationship may have been between Jesus and James and John. When listing the women who stood around the cross at the crucifixion of Christ, we find the mother of James and Joses (that is Mary the mother of Jesus, see Mt. 13:55) and the mother of Zebedee's children (James and John who is known as Salome (Mk. 15:40), but in John's gospel the list does not include Salome (the mother of James and John) but instead Mary (Jesus' mother) and her sister (Jn. 19:25). If the mother of James and John was the sister to Mary the mother of Jesus, then Jesus and James and John were first cousins. This could explain why the mother of James and John was so bold to come to Jesus and request that they sit at his right and left in his kingdom (Mt. 20:20,21). Her request seemed unusually bold, but if she was Aunt Salome, she may have felt her sons, as family, should have a special place of privilege.

Of the twelve that were chosen to be apostles, three of them occupied a special place of privilege with Jesus. Simon Peter, James, and John were allowed to follow Jesus to Jairus' house when his daughter was raised from the dead (Mk. 5:37). The same three were on the Mount of Transfiguration with Jesus (Mt. 17:1) and it was these three that accompanied Jesus in the Garden of Gethsemane (Mk. 14:32,33).

Choosing twelve from the many disciples that followed Jesus was a very important decision not to be taken lightly. It was only after spending all night in prayer (Lk. 6:12) that Jesus then called these twelve men and separated them to occupy a place of privilege and responsibility. These men would have the responsibility of carrying the message of the gospel to the nations, and yet these twelve would not have been the most logical candidates.

Two of the least likely would have been Matthew (Levi) and Simon the Zealot. The idea that these two could occupy the same room without fighting each other would almost be miraculous in itself. Matthew (Levi) was a tax collector or publican. He was employed by the government of Rome to collect taxes from Jews who were then under the dominion of the Roman Empire.

It was a common practice for kings and rulers who conquered other nations to employ people of that nation to collect taxes and tribute money and fees from their subjects. The idea of a Jew paying his taxes to a Jew instead of his Gentile ruler was supposed to make the process seem less painful and minimize riots and rebellion. However, many of the Jews looked down on the tax collectors (publicans) as traitors who sold out to their enemies. The publicans also had a reputation for collecting more tax or tribute than the Romans required to line their own pockets. The most well-known of the tax collectors was Zacchaeus, the chief publican (Lk. 19:1-10). After receiving Jesus into his house, Zacchaeus told Jesus, "Lord, the half of my goods I give to the poor, and if I have taken any thing from any man by false accusation, I restore him fourfold" (Lk. 19:8). Taking more tax than required was the practice of the day, and that is why, like Zacchaeus, the tax collectors were rich (Lk. 19:2).

Having a despised publican on his ministry team may have caused many to question Jesus, but adding a Zealot like Simon to work together with a publican was unthinkable. The Zealots were the underground militia group of the day. Their purpose was to overthrow the Romans by any means, and anyone who worked in concert with the Romans would have also been a target for their hatred and murderous desires. Bringing a Zealot and a publican together would have appeared foolish to any reasonable observer, but Jesus did not choose these men by logical reasoning. It was after spending all night in prayer and hearing the voice of his Father that he chose these men. Truly, none of Jesus' disciples carried the pedigree or educational accomplishments that would attract the learned or elite. They were all Galileans, as was Jesus himself, who were looked down on by the more orthodox Jews of Judea.

Jesus and His Disciples at Nazareth

Jesus returned to his hometown where he grew up. Nazareth was a small village of maybe 120 people. Families lived for generations in the same location, and this small town of Nazareth was no different. Apparently, this was the home of both Joseph and Mary and their many relatives. These family members and neighbors would have known all about Jesus who used to read every Sabbath day in the local synagogue.

The Sabbath day's service included prayers and several readings, one from the Torah and another from the Prophets, followed by an explanation of these verses, and possibly a translation into Aramaic, and then a sermon.

When Jesus lived in Nazareth, it was customary for him to read from the scriptures (Lk. 4:16). He also taught in this synagogue, astounding the hearers with his knowledge and understanding (Mt. 13:54, Mk. 6:2).

Upon his return to Nazareth, Jesus went to the synagogue on the Sabbath day, and they handed him the scroll of Isaiah. When he stood to read, he searched for a certain passage of scripture from the scroll, and when he found it, he read, "The Spirit of the Lord is upon me, because he has anointed me to preach the gospel to the poor; he sent me to heal the brokenhearted, to preach deliverance to the captives, and recovering of sight to the blind, to set at liberty them that are bruised, To preach the acceptable year to the Lord," (Lk. 4:18,19). After reading this passage, Jesus closed the scroll, handed it to the minister, and sat down.

When the reading of scripture was concluded, it was customary for the rabbi to sit and teach those who had heard the reading. When Jesus sat down, it was an indication that he was ready to teach them from this passage of scripture, and "the eyes of all them that were in the synagogue were fastened on him" (Lk. 4:20). As the people intently listened, Jesus began to teach them by saying, "This day is this scripture fulfilled in your ears" (Lk. 4:21). The gospel does not record what else Jesus said that day, but it was certain that he told them of the anointing that was upon him to fulfill the "acceptable year of the Lord" (Lk. 4:19).

The "acceptable year of the Lord" is the year of Jubilee. In the Book of Leviticus, this fifty-year celebration is described (Lev. 25:8-22). Israel was to number 49 years, and then, on the tenth day of the seventh month on the Day of Atonement, the Jubilee trumpet would sound, and liberty would be proclaimed throughout the land. This was the beginning of the fiftieth-year, which marked the return of every man to his inheritance. Prisoners would be released. Those who became slaves because of debt or who had sold their family's property could return and reclaim all they had previously lost. It was a time of release and restoration for everyone to begin again, debt free, recovering lost inheritances from past failures.

This Jubilee was an example of what the Messiah would accomplish when he arrived. Let's look at some of the things Jesus the Messiah would accomplish that are described in the Jubilee.

First of all, the Jubilee began on the Day of Atonement. This was the only time of the year when the high priest could enter the Most Holy place in the Tabernacle or later enter the Temple with the blood of the sacrifice. The blood of the sacrifice was sprinkled on the mercy seat on the Ark of the Covenant, which represented the very throne of God. Once the blood was applied, the Jubilee trumpet would sound declaring the year of liberty.

In the Book of Hebrews, we are told that the blood of animals could never be an adequate sacrifice, but only a foreshadowing of the work of Christ. By his own blood, he entered once into the holy place and obtained eternal redemption for us (Heb. 9:11-15). Just as the trumpet declared the Jubilee at the beginning of that fiftieth year, so Jesus sent disciples into "all the world" to trumpet or declare that liberty had come to all who believe. Prisoners were released, and the brokenhearted were healed, and inheritances, lost because of sin, were again restored. The curse of sin was defeated because of Jesus' victory over death, having fully satisfied the required judgment of God upon the cross. When Jesus came out of the tomb, it was as when the high priest came out of the holy place, having completed the sacrifice. In both cases, the time to declare liberty to the people had come.

Second, the year of Jubilee was preceded by the Sabbath year when they were not to plant crops or work in the field. God promised to bless them in the sixth year with such abundance that they would not need to harvest a crop in the seventh year but would rest that year and allow their land to rest. If they would only trust God, he would give them such abundance on the sixth year that it would last three years. By obeying God and not planting the seventh year, they would actually gain a year of harvest. The abundance of the sixth year would not only supply enough for the seventh year, but it would last until the harvest of the ninth year (Lev. 25:19-22). In this Sabbath year of rest, we see that man's provision and blessing does not come by his manual labor, but by his trust in God's work to provide all he needs. Similarly, the provision and blessing of God comes to us by faith in the redemptive work of Christ and not through any work we could accomplish for our salvation.

The year of Jubilee is described in Isaiah 49:7-12. Here the prophet describes the rejection of the Messiah, which was to be followed by kings and princes coming to worship in the "acceptable time" and in the "day of salvation". The one rejected by the people will be "preserved" and "helped" by God who gives him for "a covenant of the people". The result will be that he will cause them to "inherit the desolate heritages" when he says to the prisoners "Go forth," and he will satisfy the thirsty, leading them to "springs of water." These verses correspond to the anointing upon the Messiah who will "proclaim the acceptable year of the Lord" (Isa. 61:1,2). These are the same verses Jesus quoted in Luke 4:18 at the synagogue in Nazareth. Then in 2 Corinthians 6:2, Paul uses these same scriptures to describe our "working together" with God as ambassadors for Christ to declare this salvation or jubilee in the "time acceptable".

When Jesus taught from these scriptures in his hometown of Nazareth, he identified himself as the Messiah. This got such a strong reaction from the congregation that they were ready to kill Jesus by throwing him off of the cliff the town was built near. The people knew Joseph and Mary and Jesus' brothers and sisters (Mk. 6:3). Their familiarity with Jesus and his family hindered them from believing that he was the Messiah, for "there he could do no mighty work". Jesus said, "a prophet is not without honor but in his own country and among his own kin, and in his own house" (Mk. 6:4). The rage and unbelief of those of his own hometown caused Jesus to leave Nazareth, never to return.

Jesus' Ministry in Capernaum Continues

Upon leaving Nazareth, Jesus returns to Capernaum by the Sea of Galilee. In Capernaum, Jesus continued to teach in the synagogue and perform many miracles. Obviously, we do not know all of the miracles Jesus did, for John declares that the world itself could not contain all of the books that could have been written of all Jesus both did and taught (Jn. 21:25). But, of the recorded miracles described in the gospels, 80% of them were done in the city of Capernaum. It is no wonder that, when Jesus prophesied of the future judgment that would fall on the cities of Galilee, Capernaum was described as "exalted into heaven" (Mt. 11:23) because of all the mighty works Jesus accomplished there.

The Sermon on the Mount

The longest discourse recorded of the teachings of Jesus is found in the Gospel of Matthew 5:1-7:27. The first twelve verses of this teaching are best known as the Beatitudes or blessings that Jesus declared to those who would "hear" and "do" what he taught them (Mt. 7:24). The Greek word used here for "blessed" carries the meaning of happy, fortunate, and well off.

Blessed (happy, fortunate, and well off) are the poor in spirit (Mt. 5:3). Many have asked, "How can the condition of being poor in spirit (literally bankrupt of spirit) be a blessing?" Jesus was not saying that this is a condition we should seek, but that the good news to those who are spiritually bankrupt is that the kingdom of heaven is available to them.

When Jesus came to the people, he brought the kingdom of God or the kingdom of heaven (these terms are used interchangeably) with him. He told the religious leaders that he cast out evil spirits by the Spirit of God, and because he did, they should know that the kingdom of God had come to them (Mt. 12:28).

The kingdom of God is described as "righteousness, peace and joy in the Holy Spirit (Rom. 14:17 NKJV). The blessings of God's kingdom that Jesus brought to the people were seen by the change in their conditions. The mourners are comforted, the meek inherit the earth (literally the "land" which is a term commonly used to describe the promised land or land of Israel's possession or inheritance), those who hunger and thirst will be filled, and the merciful will obtain mercy. The blessings continue for the "pure in heart," for they will "see" or "perceive" or "know" God, and when they are persecuted and reviled and falsely accused, their heavenly reward will be great.

As the multitudes filled the hillside, Jesus taught them about the heart of God and his desire to bless and comfort them, even when the conditions are difficult. God's righteousness, peace, and joy are the conditions found in his kingdom. These conditions supersede any current circumstances we may be experiencing at the moment.

Jesus continued his discourse to the multitudes, revealing to them their value to the kingdom of God as salt and light. They were to see themselves as the preservative of society just as salt is the preservative of food. They were also to see themselves as the light or that which reveals who God is to the world. Their good works in the name of the Lord would cause others to see God's love and goodness so that praise and thanksgiving would be directed toward God. Our good works are to give demonstration of who God is and what he is like so that people will recognize him just as Nicodemus did when he came to Jesus, acknowledging, "for no man can do these miracles that you do, except God be with him" (Jn. 3:2).

The sermon on the hillside continues as Jesus begins to show the people that God is more interested in the condition of their hearts than he is in their white knuckled obedience to the law. Jesus announced, "the law says, 'You shall not murder,' but I say to you, 'Do not be angry, hateful, and ready to drag your brother to court" (Mt. 5:21,22 my paraphrase). The people could keep the law of not murdering someone, which is a physical act, but they could still be guilty before God because of their hatred toward another. After all, if their hearts were not filled with hatred, then they would have no desire for murder. They should keep the law because their hearts are right, thus, becoming like their Father in heaven.

The importance of our right relationship with one another is emphasized in the next few verses about bringing our gifts to the altar (which has to do with our worship of God) and then remembering that someone has something against us. Before we can sincerely worship God, we must attempt to be at peace with each other. We should follow Jesus' instructions in the Sermon on the Mount. He said, "Leave your gift before the altar, and go your way; first be reconciled to your brother, and then come and offer your gift" (Mt. 5:24). Our vertical worship requires our horizontal relationships be without offense. Jesus continues his instructions with the following advise.

> "Settle matters quickly with your adversary who is taking you to court. Do it while you are still together on the way, or your adversary may hand you over to the judge, and the judge may hand you over to the officer, and you may be thrown into prison. Truly I tell you, you will not get out until you have paid the last penny" (Mt. 5:25,26 NIV).

This verse sounds very similar to the eighteenth chapter of Matthew where Peter is asking Jesus about the requirements for forgiving others. Peter offered a suggestion of forgiving someone seven times (Mt. 18:21) which was probably in reference to Jesus' teaching about forgiveness recorded in Luke's gospel, "And if he trespass against [you] seven times in a day, and seven times in a day turn again to [you], saying, I repent: [you] shall forgive him" (Lk. 17:4). Peter must have been counting the offenses of one of the other disciples and was nearing the seventh time and looked to Jesus to confirm that he had fulfilled what was required. But Jesus gave him an unexpected response, "I do not say to you, up to seven times, but, up to seventy times seven" (Mt. 18:22 NKJV). In other words, forgiveness is a condition of the heart not a legal fulfillment of a law. Jesus continued to explain forgiveness in a parable of one man being forgiven much, but refused to forgive someone else even a small amount. That man's unwillingness to forgive caused him to end up in a prison of torment until he paid the price required for his release (Mt. 18:21-35).

We have all met people, even perfect strangers, who strike up a conversation with us, and within minutes, we have heard of the wrong someone did to them years before and the hardship it has caused them. Instead of forgiving the wrong done to them, they carry the torment of their unwillingness to forgive and the tormentors will continue to trouble them until they have paid the price for their deliverance, which is forgiveness. Forgiveness is not dependent on feelings. We do not have to feel like forgiving someone; we just have to do it because it is what Jesus said.

Many people get trapped in the place of believing they cannot forgive because they still have hostile emotions against the offender, but Jesus explained forgiveness is not based on emotion but on simple obedience to this command, regardless how we may feel. When Jesus taught his disciples to forgive, even seven times in the same day, their response was, "Lord, Increase our faith" (Lk. 17:5). They were saying to Jesus, we can't do that unless you give us something we do not currently possess. In response to them, Jesus said, that it doesn't matter how you feel about it; you just do it. The following is a parable Jesus used to show them they could forgive.

> But which of you, having a servant plowing or feeding cattle, will say unto him by and by, when he is come from the field, Go and sit down to meat? And will not rather say unto him, Make ready wherewith I may sup, and gird yourself, and serve me, till I have eaten and drunken; and afterward thou shall eat and drink? Doeth he thank that servant because he did the things that were commanded him? I trow not. So likewise, ye, when ye shall have done all those things which are commanded you, say, We are unprofitable servants: we have done that which was our duty to do (Lk. 17:7-10).

In this story the servant has been hard at work, in the field, all day long. When he comes in to the house at the end of the day, the master of the house does not say, "Oh your tired. Go sit down and rest and eat," but instead his master says, "Fix me something to eat; serve me first, and then you can eat and rest." The servant does not feel like serving his master after he has worked all day, but he does it because it is required of him. Jesus told his disciples this is how they were to forgive. They did not need more faith; they just needed to choose to forgive because it was what was required of them. Their attitude was to be, "We have done that which was our duty to do."

The sermon on the hillside continues as Jesus again compares outward deeds to the condition of the heart. Under the Law of Moses, adultery was a capital offense. But Jesus said, "…whosoever looks on a woman to lust after her hath committed adultery with her already in his heart" (Mt. 5:28). This precedes an admonition to pluck out your right eye or cut off your right hand if that is what is required to restrain you from sin (Mt. 5:29,30). This saying is a figure of speech or a Jewish idiom. Jesus is not suggesting that people mutilate their bodies, for plucking out your right eye and cutting off your right hand does not forbid that person from lusting with their left eye or sinning with their left hand. If a man sees an attractive woman and allows his lustful heart to fuel his imagination, he may attempt to fulfill the deed of adultery. His eye is the member of his body that sees, and his hand represents his deeds, but if his heart is right, being free from lust, he will keep himself from sin. He will "cut off" the work of adultery, not because he is blind or physically impaired, but because his heart is right before God. Again, the emphasis is on the condition of the heart, not just outward obedience.

Continuing, Jesus makes mention of divorce, "It hath been said, Whosoever shall put away his wife, let him give her a writing of divorcement: But I say unto you, That whosoever shall put away his wife, saving for the cause of fornication, causeth her to commit adultery: and whosoever shall marry her that is divorced committeth adultery" (Mt. 5:31,32). This is not an exhaustive teaching on remarriage and divorce by Jesus and unfortunately this portion of scripture has been misunderstood to condemn almost all divorce and any marriage to someone who has been divorced. Fortunately, we have other scriptures that help clarify Jesus' remarks.

The Pharisees came to Jesus, tempting him to say something that would violate the Law of Moses so that they could accuse him (Mt. 19:3). Yes, Moses gave them permission to divorce, but the religious leaders had perverted the conditions of divorce so thoroughly that they include almost anything about wives that displeased their husbands. Burning the toast or scaring the camels may be examples that are a little too extreme, but the idea here is that, any time a man's wife displeased him, he could divorce her. According to Matthew, "They said unto him. Why did Moses then command to give a writing of divorcement, and to put her away?" (19:7). Jesus explained the reason for their divorcing was the hardness of their hearts (Mt. 19:8). In the Gospel of Mark, chapter 10, verses eleven and twelve also reports that Jesus explains that the primary reason for divorce is unfaithfulness, but in Matthew the idea here is made even clearer.

If I divorce my wife to marry another married woman, I cause her (the married woman) to commit adultery, and I commit adultery by marrying a divorced woman who left her husband for me. I do not cause my original wife to commit adultery by my divorcing her as some have said. Jesus is actually dealing again with the heart. "Because of he hardness of your heart" was his reply to the Pharisees. Jesus brought them back to God's original intention, asking, "Have ye not read, that he which made them at the beginning made them male and female, And said, For this cause shall a man leave father and mother, and shall cleave to his wife: and they twain shall be one flesh?" (Mt. 19:4,5). The husband was to "cleave" (literally weld together) to his wife, and thereby they would become one.

Paul teaches both the Corinthians and Ephesians the purpose of marriage and the reasons for the provision of divorce (1 Cor. 7:1-16, 26-40; Eph. 5:22-33). God's will is for marriage to exemplify the relationship of the Church to Christ: our total love and devotion to him and his unwavering love for us. Again, it is a matter of the heart. Paul writes, "Wives, submit yourselves unto your own husbands, as unto the Lord" (Eph. 5:22), and later adds, "Husbands, love your wives, even as Christ also loved the church, and gave himself for it (Eph. 5:,25).

Jesus' sermon continues with various topics. The next is in regards to swearing, trying to convince those who hear that you are telling the truth (Mt. 5:33-37). It may be like children who tell their playmates, "cross my heart and hope to die." It is an attempt to cause others to believe that you are telling the truth. Jesus' response in this passage is simply to always tell the truth. - Let your…Yes be yes and your no be no (Mt. 5:37 NKJV). We should not have to bind ourselves to a curse in order to prove that our words are truthful.

The next section deals with retaliation (Mt. 5:38-48). The words of Jesus about not resisting evil should not be understood as indicating that we are to just lie down and let the devil run all over us. We have plenty of other scriptures that tell us, "Resist the devil, and he will flee from you" (James 4:7). Instead, Jesus is teaching about retaliating against someone who has harmed us or caused us trouble. It should not be that we react to evil with evil. We should react to evil with the love of God instead. Jesus is not making a case against self-defense here. He is telling us not to attempt to "get even" by doing harm to those who harmed us. Turning the other cheek, giving more than required, removes any doubt about our intentions.

According to the laws of Rome, a soldier could conscript a man to carry his backpack for one mile. Even if a Jewish man were walking west on the road and he met a Roman soldier heading east, the Jewish man could be compelled to carry the soldier's pack, but once the mile requirement had been met, the Jewish man could fling down the pack, probably accompanied with some choice words of disdain, before continuing his westward journey. But, Jesus told his listeners that, if they were compelled to go one mile, they should go two instead. Thus, he indicated that we should do more than just that which is required. Consequently, the expected animosity is removed and an opportunity to demonstrate the love of God is presented. To love our enemies, to bless them who curse us and to do good to them that hate us and despitefully use us and persecute us is uncommon, but if we do these things, then we shall be like our Father in heaven. Loving those who love us and blessing those who bless us is easy and is practiced even by those who do not know the love of God. As children of our heavenly Father, we are to accurately represent him by "being perfect, even as [our] Father which is in heaven is perfect" (Mt. 5:48).

The next chapter of Matthew's gospel continues this discourse by Jesus as he deals with giving to the poor, praying, and fasting. Once again, the emphasis is on the attitude of the heart, not the public demonstration that solicits the praises of men.

Jesus admonished his listeners that, when they gave to the poor, they should not give "as the hypocrites do in the synagogues and in the streets, that they [might] have glory of men" (Mt. 6:2). This practice of the Jewish religious leaders has been described like this: a servant of the Jewish leader, standing on the street corner and blowing a trumpet gets everyone's attention. He then proceeds to proclaim, "the holy man of God gives alms to the poor," and reaching into the money pouch, he pulls out coins to distribute to those who have gathered around. Jesus said that the only reward they would receive was from those who admire their public generosity. Jesus continued, "but when you give alms, do not let your left hand know what your right hand does" (Mt. 6:3). In other words, give to those in need without anyone else knowing about it, and then God, your Father, will reward you publicly.

This same principle is repeated regarding praying and fasting. To pray publicly for a prideful purpose or to let everyone know you are fasting to gain the reputation as someone who is religious or "holy" has only limited reward. The only reward for such public displays is the acclaim of the people who see these "pious" activities. The true purpose of prayer and fasting is not to receive approval of man, but to please God. God's reward for the righteous secret prayer is revealed when the answer to that prayer comes publicly (Mt. 6:18).

We know from Paul's letter to the Church at Ephesus that there are many kinds of prayers. He writes, "Keep on praying in the Spirit, with every kind of prayer and entreaty" (Eph. 6:18 Williams). Jesus, in this discourse, addresses several vital aspects regarding prayer. He instructs his listeners saying, "After this manner therefore pray" (Mt. 6:9):

> "Our Father in heaven,
> Hallowed be Your name.
> Your kingdom come.
> Your will be done
> On earth as it is in heaven.
> Give us this day our daily bread.
> And forgive us our debts,
> As we forgive our debtors.
> And do not lead us into temptation,
> But deliver us from the evil one.
> For Yours is the kingdom and the power and the glory forever.
> Amen" (Mt. 6:9-13 NKJV).

This prayer, often referred to as the Lord's Prayer, would be better described as the model prayer. This is an outline for praying as Jesus described earlier. The components of this kind of prayer include: Praise and adoration, calling for the kingdom of God to come and the will of God to be done on earth as it is in heaven, daily provision, forgiveness of sins in proportion to our forgiving others, preservation from temptation and evil, and the acknowledgment of God's eternal kingdom and power.

The expansion and flexibility of this prayer outline is almost limitless. It allows the one praying to be led by the Holy Spirit instead of being limited to a form.

Hallowing (to make holy or consecrate, honor as holy) the name of God reminds us of who God is and what he is like and who he is to us personally. In the scriptures, God is called by many different names, each revealing a different aspect of his character. Obviously, when Jesus was teaching this, there were no New Testament scriptures, so Jesus was referencing the Law, the Psalms, and the Prophets that describe the names of God.

We know from Moses that the personal name of God is Jehovah (YWHW), and in the scriptures there are eight compound names of Jehovah, each describing a different aspect of God's character. The following is a list of those names in Hebrew:

Jehovah-Tsidkenu	The Lord our righteousness	Jer. 23:6
Jehovah-M'Kaddesh	The Lord our sanctification	Lev. 20:8; Ex. 31:13
Jehovah-Shalom	The Lord our peace	Judges 6:24
Jehovah-Shammah	The Lord who is present	Ezek. 48:35
Jehovah-Rapha	The Lord our healer	Ex. 15:26
Jehovah-Jireh	The Lord our provider*	Gen. 22:14
Jehovah-Rohi	The Lord our shepherd	Ps. 23
Jehovah-Nissi	The Lord our banner	Ex. 17:15

(* Literally the Lord who "sees" i.e. looks ahead and sees the need and makes provision ahead of time).

Honoring God by acknowledging that God is our: righteousness, our sanctification, our peace, our healer, provider, shepherd and banner, as well as, always being present with us should help us begin our day praising God because these characteristics are who he is to us and for us.

Praising God with his redemptive names is to be followed by proclaiming the will of God to be done in the earth as it is done in heaven. God's will is always done in heaven, but God's will is not always done in the earth.

Some may have a different opinion regarding the events on earth, believing they are always in accordance to the sovereign will of the Almighty. However, it does not require much study of scripture to see that much of what goes on in the earth is far from the will of God. Murder, adultery, falsehood, stealing, etc. are forbidden in heaven and are condemned on earth, but that does not prevent people from engaging in these activities daily. The "thou shall not's" of the law are the will of God so how can some say because God is sovereign his will is always done? This would make God the author of sin. In actuality, the will of God is not always done on earth but is seldom done . Therefore, the exhortation to pray this way is not just a religious idea, but is a directive to stand in the authority God gave us, in the name of Jesus, commanding his will to be done and his kingdom to come.

Now we are to pray for our daily provision. "Give us this day" foreshadows the later teaching Jesus gives in this sermon about the birds and the flowers that do not sow or reap, and yet God takes care of their daily needs. This statement is followed by a question, "Are you not much better than they?" (Mt. 7:26). The implied answer is yes; man is more important than the rest of God's creation. Man was made to rule on earth, having dominion over all of God's creation. If God is aware of the number of hairs on our head (Lk. 12:7) or even when a sparrow falls to the ground (Mt. 10:29), he is certainly knowledgeable of our current circumstances. One of the very names of God, Jehovah-Jireh, is his promise to provide what we need and to remind us of his ability to do so even when it is impossible to farm our ground and wait for the harvest.

Forgiving others is the next segment of this prayer outline. We are to forgive those who are in debt or who have sinned against us.

Matthew's record uses the word "debts" while Luke's account uses the word "sin" (Mt. 6:12, Lk. 11:4). The Greek word in Matthew's account is translated debt, meaning, "that which is owed" or metaphorically, "offense or sin", while Luke uses the most commonly translated word for offense or sin. I believe the use of these two words is significant in that to forgive someone is an obligation; it is that which we owe or is due to someone else. They may be the offender, the source of our trouble or pain, yet forgiveness is what we owe them. It is not optional. Until we pay our debt of forgiveness to the one who has hurt, wounded, or offended us, we are under the judgment of the courts of heaven and cannot be cleared of our debt until we fulfill that obligation.

Those who have never experienced the forgiveness of God cannot understand how offenders have any right to receive forgiveness from the ones they offended. It does not make sense to the natural mind. However, to those who know God's forgiveness, this truth demonstrates what they have experienced. God has forgiven man, who stands guilty before him, but is forgiven anyway. This forgiveness is not based on man's works to right his wrongs but only on God's mercy and personal sacrifice that carried our sins to the cross and forgave all who put him there. Christ's persecutors were not only the Roman soldiers who drove the nails into his body, but every man, woman, and child who has ever sinned. No one is exempt from this guilt, but all are forgiven. Forgiveness is owed to us because the price for forgiveness was paid in full. Therefore, we must forgive those who have sinned against us.

The phrase "Lead us not into temptation" is worded the same in both of the gospels that record this prayer. The words to lead may conjure up the picture of a shepherd leading his sheep into a place of temptation (testing, tribulation, trouble). Some have even suggested that God leads his people into temptation or trouble just to test them, to see how they do under pressure. Fortunately, doctrines are not to be determined by man's understanding of one scripture. The

Good Shepherd leads his sheep into green pastures and beside still waters (Ps. 23). These are places of abundance and peace. James tells us about this very idea of accusing God of bringing temptation into our lives when he writes,

"Let no man say when he is tempted, I am tempted of God: for God cannot be tempted with evil, neither tempteth he any man" (James 1:13). Obviously, temptations (testing's, trials, and troubles) come to everyone, but both the source of temptations and the promise of blessing to the overcomers are also spoken of in the Book of James. Temptation comes as a result of man's lusts when he is drawn away and enticed to sin because of the desires of the flesh (James 1:14,15).

James assures us, however, that "the one who endures (perseveres) temptation… shall receive the crown of life…" (1:12). We are to rule in life (Rom. 5:17). The crown is placed on the head of the king (the one who rules). We are to rule over temptations when they come our way. When we overcome the temptation of the flesh, we continue to rule in the realm of life. The words "Lead us, **not** into temptation, **but** deliver us from evil" in no way imply that God just might lead us into trouble. Instead, these words should be our prayer to keep us from yielding to our flesh and consequently entering into temptation and bring trouble into our lives.

I don't think the instruction Jesus gives us in this list of prayer topics is just a random order. Instead, I think it is very significant that the warning of temptation to follow our flesh (senses, feelings) follows the command to forgive those who have sinned against us. The request, "Forgive us, as we forgive others and lead us not into temptation, but deliver us from evil" seems to me to emphasize the necessity of forgiving an offence, even when we do not "feel" (flesh) like we can or even want to. Even after the "Amen" of this model prayer, Jesus continues to emphasize forgiveness. He announces. "For if you forgive men their trespasses, your heavenly Father will also forgive you: But if you forgive not men their trespasses, neither will your Father forgive your trespasses" (Mt. 6:14,15). How can God forgive us of not forgiving another, as long as we choose to remain in that place where we have exalted the sin of another to be greater than the sacrifice of Jesus? He can't do it. The blood of Jesus cleanses from all sin, not just yours and mine, but all those that may have sinned against us.

The conclusion of this model prayer is a declaration of God's eternal kingdom, power, and glory. God's kingdom is an everlasting kingdom, and God's glory shall fill all the earth. His power is greater than all powers. These words of adulation are not just the concluding of a prayer, but a reminder that we are not in some temporary condition limited to our lifetime. This kingdom is eternal and ever increasing, and we will participate in it as members of God's own family both now and forever. "Of the increase of his government and peace there shall be no end" (Isa. 9:7).

Jesus' Discourse Continues

Once again Jesus is calling the attention of those listening to the condition of their heart (spirit and soul) and what is most valuable. The things we treasure the most should be found in heaven and not on earth. The storing up of goods for the future is certainly not forbidden or discouraged, for much of the Book of Proverbs tell us how to wisely conduct our lives so that our "barns are filled with plenty and our presses burst forth with new wine" (Prov. 3:10). But, the problem with earthly treasures is that moth and rust can corrupt them and thieves can break in and steal them (Mt. 6:19). It is the "love of money" that "is the root of all evil" (1 Tim. 6:10), and what we love is where we find our treasure (Mt. 6:21).

This admonition to fill our hearts with the treasures of heaven is followed by Jesus talking about an eye that is "single" (sound, whole, good). To have a good eye is to have good sight. To have an evil eye is to have a diseased or blind eye that leaves you in the dark. But this is more than just having the ability to see with your physical eyes because Jesus continues to say, "if therefore the light that is in [you] be darkness, how great is that darkness" (Mt. 6:23). In Paul's letter to the Ephesians, he gives a definition of light, "for whatsoever doth make manifest is light" (Eph. 5:13). Not only is light necessary for our physical eyes to function, but is often used to describe a mental or spiritual revelation or understanding. For instance, the psalmist writes, "The entrance of Your words gives light; it gives understanding to the simple" (Ps. 119:130 NKJV). Similarly, darkness or blindness is often associated with obscurity or ignorance. John tells us in his first epistle, "He who loves his brother abides in the light, and there is no occasion of stumbling in him. But he that hates his brother is in darkness and walks in darkness, and does not know where he is going, because that darkness has blinded his eyes" (1 Jn. 2:10,11 NKJV). It is clear that we should walk in love if we want to receive the light of understanding.

Without pause, Jesus continues teaching about the impossibility of serving two masters because a person can only love one at a time. The "masters" here are identified as God and wealth (mammon). While this topic may seem to be unrelated to the point of the previous verses, they are really all connected.

We lay up treasures (things we love) in our hearts. The things we love (treasure) are the things we see (perceive) as most valuable. That perception (sight) will either bring us light (understanding, revelation) or darkness (ignorance, blindness). What we love (treasure) is what we serve (God or earthly wealth). If we serve earthly treasures, they will be subject to corruption and theft. If we serve God, our treasures cannot be stolen and will never corrupt or decay. The remainder of this chapter deals with this same subject. Worry, fear, anxiety over having enough food and drink, clothes to wear, and a place to live is a cruel master. Fearing the loss of these things is a tormenting condition. If we serve these things, then they are what rule over us, occupy our thoughts, and control the way we perceive life. Consequently, we are to think differently by looking at (seeing, perceiving) God's faithful provision that extends even to birds and flowers. We must all ask ourselves this question: "If God takes care of the birds and flowers, won't he also take care of me?" The answer to this question for each one of us is a resounding "Yes!" and should bring us great comfort. If we know that seeking God and putting our trust in his faithfulness will result in our daily provision, we need never choose to let worry, fear, or anxiety be our master.

This final section of the sermon on the hillside is a contrast between carnal and spiritual people. Measuring out judgment to another will only cause that same judgment to return upon us. Some of us observe tiny specks or splinters of imperfections in someone else but are oblivious to the timber-sized flaws in our own life. Jesus instructs us to first deal with our personal imperfections and failings. Once we have been successful in removing the blindness that was obscuring our own vision, we may then see clearly to help others (Mt. 7:1-5).

Both dogs and swine were considered unclean and to be avoided by the Jews of Jesus' time, and this knowledge helps us to understand that giving what is holy to dogs or casting pearls to the swine (Mt. 7:6) are obviously metaphorical expressions. They mean that the things that are consecrated to God and precious to us as believers will not be honored or valued by unbelievers. Those with no ability to understand spiritual things are as dogs or swine that would only destroy the precious things of God and treat them as foolishness (1 Cor. 2:14). Titus makes a similar observation when he tells us "Unto the pure all things are pure: but unto them that are defiled and unbelieving is nothing pure; but even their mind and conscience is defiled" (1:15). Jesus' comparisons are not a slanderous name calling against those who have not yet believed. They are instructions for us who do understand, to correctly handle those personal revelations that God gives to us as his children. The "love notes" in the lunch box will probably not be understood by the neighbor's kids (Mt. 7:6).

The goodness of God is described in terms of fatherhood. If we, as parents, will only give good things to our children, how much more will God, our Father, only give good things to those who ask him? A parent who would give a son or daughter a snake or a rock (something that might harm them) instead of bread and fish (a typical meal of that day) would be considered cruel and unloving. Children are often relentless in their asking for something they want. We, as children of God, are encouraged to continue to ask, seek, and knock until we have obtained what we requested. This is not begging God or pestering God, hoping he will get tired of our ceaseless pleading and give us what we want. No, this is continually asking, seeking, and persistently knocking until we receive the things that God has purposed for us to receive, the good things of God. We are not then to be careless with these good things, but as good stewards over what God has entrusted to us, we should do for others what we would want them to do for us. The love and generosity we show to others is fulfilling the will of God (Mt. 7:7-12).

There are roads we should travel and places we should strive to enter, as well as paths to avoid and places we should not go. The "wide... gate" and "broad... way" (Mt. 7:13) speak of the common, the thoughtless, the "go with the herd" mentality that leads to ruin, despair, and trouble. The "strait... and narrow...way" (Mt. 7:14) relays the idea of a small opening, a narrow entrance where those who pass through must go in a single file to enter. This entrance is guarded, and proper credentials are required, but the one who gets access finds life. However, proper credentials are not offered to just an elite few. The door is always open, and everyone is invited to enter without cost. Jesus said, "I am the door: by me if any man enter in, he shall be saved, and shall go in and out, and find pasture" (Jn. 10:9). Another translation of this scripture says, "I am the Gateway. To enter through me is to experience life, freedom, and satisfaction"

(Jn. 10:9 TPT). This is not some hidden doorway, obscured from public view, but a well-lit pathway where wisdom cries aloud to all who would hear and enter (Pr. 1:20-23). The Way is plain, but narrow. Jesus said, "I am the way, the truth, and the life: no man comes to the Father, but by me" (Jn. 14:6). Through Jesus, we all can have the proper credentials to enter the life that only he gives. Maybe that is why the next few verses warn us of false prophets.

False prophets are those who speak a word in the name of the Lord, but their purpose and their prophecies are false. They are described as wolves in sheep's clothing (Mt. 7:15). The Scriptures often refer to God's people as sheep, Psalm 100 declares that "we are his [God's] people, and the sheep of his pasture" (verse 3). The tenth chapter of John's gospel reveals Jesus as the "Good Shepherd" of the sheep who "gives his life for the sheep" (Jn. 10:11,14). We are the sheep, and Jesus is our shepherd.

Wolves are natural predators to sheep so the false prophets come to "steal, and to kill, and to destroy" (Jn. 10:10). They are dressed as sheep to deceive and ultimately destroy those who would listen to their false prophecies. Fortunately, the promise of Jesus is that his sheep hear his voice and follow him and the "stranger will they not follow…for they know not the voice of strangers" (Jn. 10:4,5). These "strangers" (false prophets) are easy to recognize because we "shall know them by their fruits" (Mt. 7:16). Because a good tree cannot produce evil fruit or an evil tree produce good fruit, a tree is known by the kind of fruit it produces. Similarly, wolves (the false prophets) are evil trees and cannot produce the fruit of the kingdom of God: "righteousness, peace and joy…" (Rom. 14:17). Only the sheep of God's pasture (the good trees) can produce the fruit of God's kingdom.

Jesus reveals that there are those who call him Lord whom he does not recognize as belonging to his kingdom. They are imposters who prophesy in the name of Jesus. They cast out demons and do wonderful works, but Jesus describes them as those who work iniquity (Mt. 7:23). Their fruit (works) reveals who they really are (wolves), those whom Jesus has never known.

The last four verses of this discourse by Jesus are a parable contrasting a wise man to a foolish man. Both of these men built a house. Both houses were exposed to the same storm of wind, rain, and flood, but only one house remained standing after the storm passed. One house survived the storm, but the other was totally destroyed. What was the difference in these two houses? The first house had an immovable foundation. The builder dug deep until he found a solid rock on which to build his house. The other builder built upon the sand, so when the storm came, it washed the sand from under the house resulting in the collapse of the house and "great was the fall of it" (Mt. 7:27).

The problem with the fallen house was not the house itself, but the foundation on which it was built. The story illustrates the necessity of building upon the right kind of foundation. Each of these houses represents the person's life. Jesus said whosoever hears and does what he says is wise (Mt. 7:26). The sayings (words) of Jesus are the solid rock foundation, and the building of the house equates to the building of our lives upon his word. Just as a physical building needs a solid rock foundation that cannot be affected by any kind of storm, so our lives must be built upon something that will last forever.

The scriptures are clear regarding the eternal nature of the Word of God. Psalm 119 says, "Forever O Lord, your word is settled in heaven" (verse 89), Jesus proclaims, "Heaven and earth shall pass away: but my words shall not pass away" (Lk. 21:33). If the word of God is eternal, immovable, and unchangeable, then it is a reliable foundation upon which to build our lives.

We have all seen houses where construction was started but never finished. I drove by a property for years that had a foundation with plumbing sticking out of the poured slab. It looked like it would have been a large and grand house, but the foundation was never built upon, and weeds in the overgrown lot eventually obscured the view of what could have been.

We may possess a copy of the Word of God. We may dress it up with a fancy cover, gold leaf the wording on the binder, and give it a place of honor in our houses, but it is only when we "do" the Word of God that we are building our lives upon that which cannot be moved. Jesus said the wise man is the one who "hears [my] sayings, and does them" (Mt. 7:24). James warns us against being merely hearers of the word of God, but not doers of that word (James 1:22). James says we are self-deceived if we only hear God's Word. It is the "doer" that is "blessed in his deed" (James 1:25).

When Jesus concluded his sermon on the hillside, his teaching astonished the people because he taught them with authority (Mt. 7:28,29). His words carried the authority of the kingdom of God and not just the platitudes of the religious leaders, scribes, and rabbis that they were so accustomed to hearing.

The Miracles Continue

Finishing his teachings, Jesus descended from the hillside accompanied by the multitudes (Mt. 8:1). In the next verse, we learn that before entering the gates to the city of Capernaum, Jesus found himself face to face with a man who was a leper. This man worshipped Jesus. The word "worshipped" here (Mt. 8:2) means he fell down and prostrated himself at Jesus' feet. This was a very bold move for a leper who was not allowed near others. The law required lepers to stand at a distance if anyone approached them and loudly declare, "unclean, unclean," warning of their condition. If lepers approached someone, they could be stoned to death, the ultimate penalty for possibly infecting others. But this man, seeing Jesus leading the multitudes, recognized his opportunity to get close to Jesus and be healed of his disease. He was willing to risk everything for a chance of being made clean. The man immediately said to Jesus, "Lord, if you will, you can make me clean" (Mt. 8:2). This statement of great faith acknowledged his faith in Jesus' ability but the leper was uncertain of Jesus' willingness to heal him.

I love what Jesus said and did. According to Matthew, he "put forth his hand, and touched him, saying, I will: be thou clean" (Mt. 8:3). Immediately, the man was cleansed of his leprosy, healed in an instant. This miraculous event requires further research found in Mark's Gospel. There, the scriptures tell us that Jesus was "moved with compassion, put forth his hand and touched him, and said to him, I will: be clean" (Mk. 1:41). The next verse reveals to us when this disease of leprosy departed from him and he was cleansed. It was when Jesus had "spoken" the words, "be clean."

Did Jesus need to touch the leper for this man to be healed? We find many examples when Jesus was nowhere near the people he healed. The noblemen's son was 20 miles away; the centurion's servant was not present, and the Syrophenician's daughter was at home, yet they were all healed from a distance when Jesus spoke. So why did Jesus touch this leper who was diseased and most likely had open sores on his body?

Jesus is touched with the feelings of our infirmities (Heb. 4:15). He knows what it is like to be "despised and rejected of men, a man of sorrows and acquainted with grief" (Isa. 53:3). Mark's gospel emphasizes that Jesus was "moved with compassion." Before him was a man who was an outcast of society, one who had lost everything because of his disease. He may not have had a human touch for years, and the pain of being identified as "unclean" must have taken its toll on him emotionally. I'm sure the multitudes behind Jesus were all objecting to the presence of this leper with cruel words of condemnation. Having leprosy carried a stigma of being a sinner and bearing the judgment of God. The compassion of Jesus moved him to touch this man. I don't believe it was an arm-length tap on the forehead kind of touch, but an all out embrace. This man needed more than physical healing; he needed to know he was forgiven, loved, and accepted by God, and he was not disappointed. Jesus hugged him, healed him, and accepted him into the multitude of followers before entering the city.

A Withered Hand Healed

On the Sabbath day, Jesus entered into the synagogue in Capernaum. There was a man with a withered hand. The reason for his malady is not made known. He may have had a stroke or became crippled as the result of some accident. When Jesus arrived at the synagogue, the scribes and Pharisees asked him, "Is it lawful to heal on the Sabbath days?" (Mt. 12:10). They were not seeking an answer from Jesus; they were looking for an opportunity to "accuse" him.

This same group of religious leaders had just challenged Jesus about the activities of his disciples, for they had seen them plucking the heads of grain* to eat as they walked through the grain* fields on the Sabbath day (Mt. 12:1; Mk. 2:23; Lk. 6:1). Jesus defended the right of his disciples to pluck and eat grain on the Sabbath by using King David as an example. David and those who were with him ate of the showbread. Doing so was unlawful for anyone except the priests. Jesus was illustrating how the needs of David (whom the Pharisees revered) and his men took precedence over the laws regarding the showbread just as the needs of the disciples superseded the Sabbath laws. Even the Pharisees would pull a sheep out of a pit it had fallen

---

*(Note: The KJV uses the term corn and corn fields; however, corn was not grown as a crop or known in ancient times except in the Western Hemisphere, particularly in Mexico. It was introduced to Europe by the Spanish explorers. The word translated "corn" can refer to many different kinds of grain, e.g. wheat, barley, rye, etc...)

into on the Sabbath. Jesus noted that certainly a person is much more valuable than a sheep (Mt. 12:11,12), so Jesus was justified in healing on the Sabbath. Jesus then punctuated his answer by saying, "The Sabbath was made for man, and not man for the Sabbath. Therefore the Son of man is Lord also of the Sabbath" (Mk. 2:27,28).

When the Pharisees questioned Jesus regarding healing on the Sabbath, his response to them was found in the instruction he gave the crippled man, "Stand" and the question he asked those in the synagogue, "Is it lawful to do good on the Sabbath days, or to do evil? to save life, or to kill?" (Mk. 3:4). The fear and intimidation the religious leaders held over those in the synagogue that kept them from answering this simple question caused Jesus to become both angered and grieved. The calloused hearts of the Pharisees would deny this crippled man his healing if it were not for Jesus' willingness to be falsely accused and threatened. Standing in the face of all opposition, Jesus commanded the man, to reach out his hand, an act which resulted in his being perfectly healed and restored.

You might expect that those who were present and witnessed such a miraculous display of God's power and goodness would have voiced their praise and thanksgiving to God and joy for this man's healing and recovery, but instead the scriptures record that the Pharisees left the synagogue to counsel with the Herodians about how they might destroy Jesus.

With the prospect of further conflict with the Pharisees, Jesus withdrew himself to the shore of the Sea of Galilee, just outside of the city of Capernaum. Not only did Jesus' disciples follow him but so did a huge crowd formed from the regions of Galilee, Judaea, from the city of Jerusalem and Idumaea, even coming from the land beyond Jordan, including the cities of Tyre and Sidon. Away from the intimidating influence of the hostile religious leaders, the people brought their sick to Jesus who healed their bodies and set them free from the oppressive, demonic work that had held them in bondage for so long (Mk. 3:7-12).

Let Down through the Roof

Again in the city of Capernaum, Jesus was teaching (Mk. 2:1; Lk. 5:17), and the crowds gathered around the house where he was staying. Mark's gospel tells us that there were so many people that it was impossible to receive them into the house. Luke's account tells us who these people were who made up this multitude; it was the Pharisees and doctors of the law who had come out of every town in Galilee, Judea, and even the city of Jerusalem. These were the religious elite who had assembled to listen to Jesus. Some had traveled from Jerusalem where the Temple was; they were undoubtedly the chief priests and rulers. Others came from Judea, the region in the south near the capital city, and then others came from the many towns and villages near Capernaum in Galilee, some sixty miles to the north of Jerusalem.

The reason for the assembly of these religious leaders is not given, but from many other accounts of Jesus' dealings with the Pharisees, it would seem that their intentions were less than friendly. Because this curious congregation had gathered, Mark tells us, Jesus, "preached the word to them" (2:2). I wonder how many experienced what Simon and Cleopas described after seeing Jesus on the road to Emmaus. They asked each other, "Did not our heart burn within us, while he talked with us by the way, and while he opened to us the scriptures?" (Lk. 24:32).

While the religious were weighing the words of Jesus, four men were carrying a crippled friend to the meeting. When they arrived at the house where Jesus was, they were not allowed to enter. No one made way for this man who needed a miracle. Once again the religious stood in the way of those in need, but that did not deter these men who were intent on bringing their friend to Jesus. They climbed up on top of the house and proceeded to break up the clay covering of the flat roof. Many houses of that day were built with four outside walls and then large timbers on top to support the roof. Above the timbers, the area was supported with smaller branches that made a nearly solid base, which was then covered with a thick layer of clay. To break up a roof like that and make an opening large enough to lower the crippled man by ropes tied to the four corners of his bed would have taken a considerable amount of time.

I have often wondered what Jesus did when pieces of the ceiling began to fall to the floor. Did he sit down and watch with the others to see what was happening? Was this twenty or thirty-minute procedure accompanied by the complaints of the owner of the house? I marvel at the ingenuity and determination of these men to get to Jesus. I wonder how many people today would be willing to destroy the roof of a building to get a friend to the one who could save him? This was obviously a work of faith because when Jesus "saw their faith" (Lk. 5:20), he responded to the crippled man. According to James, real faith has corresponding action (2:17), and the actions of these men showed Jesus their confidence in him to heal their friend.

Neither the man, his friends, nor the gathering of religious leaders, expected what Jesus said to the crippled man. Instead of addressing his illness, Jesus looked at him and said, "Man, your sins are forgiven you" (Lk. 5:20 NKJV). The scribes and Pharisees immediately began to think that Jesus was speaking blasphemies, for no one had the authority to forgive sins except God. No one said a word, but Jesus perceived their thoughts and challenged them to judge which is easier, to forgive sins or to heal the lame. Before they even had time to answer, Jesus said to the crippled man, "Arise, take up your bed, and go to your house" (Lk. 5:24 NKJV). Immediately the man arose and picked up the bed he was carried in and left the house praising God. The authority Jesus had to forgive sins was demonstrated in the power to heal the sick. Jesus and his disciples then left the house, and the religious leaders were amazed and filled with fear. The crippled man was the only one healed that day even though the "power of the Lord was present to heal them" (Lk. 5:17). The power of God was present to heal everybody in the house, and surely there were many among those who gathered who needed healing, but only the one who was forgiven received a miracle. Faith received from God while the reasoning and judgment of the pious left them fearful and bewildered.

THE CENTURION'S FAITH

Once again Jesus left the city and taught the multitudes along the coasts of the Sea of Galilee and in the synagogues of their towns and villages. Upon returning to Capernaum, Jesus was greeted by the elders of the Jews who began begging him to come and heal the servant of a certain centurion. The Roman officer had enlisted the help of the Jewish leadership to persuade Jesus to heal one of his servants who was sick and nearly dead (Lk. 7:1-10). Although the Jewish leaders were not usually friendly with Jesus, they felt obliged to accommodate this man who had paid for the building of their synagogue in Capernaum. This Roman must have been a man of some wealth because the synagogue in Capernaum had the reputation of being one of the most beautiful in all of Galilee.

As the Jews approached Jesus, they tried to extol the goodness of this Roman by convincing Jesus that this man, "Loves our nation and has built us a synagogue" and, therefore, was "worthy." This Roman may have been a Jewish proselyte, i.e. one who believed and worshipped the God of Israel but who had not been circumcised or who did not ritually keep the Law of Moses. We see that Luke suggests this because when Jesus approached the house, the centurion sent others to tell Jesus that he was unworthy for Jesus to "enter under [his] roof." Under rabbinical law, it was prohibited for a Jewish man to enter the house of a Gentile. In fact, Peter needed an open vision to convince him that it was all right for him to enter the house of Cornelius (Acts 10:28). Jesus was willing to go to the Gentile's house, but the centurion must have considered his request unreasonable and sent others to Jesus. This is when the true faith of this Roman is revealed. His message to Jesus was, "I am not worthy that you should enter under my roof. Therefore I did not even think myself worthy to come unto You. But say the. word, and my servant will be healed" (Lk. 7:6,7 NKJV). The centurion continues by explaining his authority over his soldiers and servants who obey his every command and his recognition of the authority Jesus carried. He acknowledged that Jesus could just command the sickness to leave his servant, and his servant would be healed.

Jesus marveled at the faith of this man. Turning to the crowd that followed him through the streets he declared, "I have not found so great faith, no, not in Israel" (Mt. 8:10). This Roman understood how authority worked. He was a Roman centurion, meaning he had command of 100 soldiers. As long as he remained under the authority of Rome ("I am a man set under authority"), he had all the authority of Rome to command those under him. His understanding of authority gave him much confidence in the authority of Jesus to give a command and heal his servant. When the friends of the centurion returned to the house, they found the servant who had been sick perfectly whole. It wasn't the worthiness of the centurion or his good works that got him his heart's desire, but his humility and faith in Jesus.

The Widow's Son of Nain

The next day Jesus and his disciples traveled to the city of Nain, a small community about 25 miles southwest of Capernaum. The meaning of Nain is pleasant or beauty and must have been a desirable place to live. Jesus did not travel there alone, but it is recorded that "many of his disciples went with him, and much people" (Lk.

7:11). Jesus was on a mission and whether or not he knew what his assignment would be that day, he followed the leading of the Spirit to the gate of the city. There, he encountered a funeral procession exiting the city and going to the place of burial. Jesus learned that the deceased was a young man, the only son of his mother and she was a widow. The overwhelming sorrow of the loss of her son was coupled with the uncertainty of this mother's future. Widows were dependent on their sons to provide for them, a responsibility that was expected and taken very seriously by all of society. With no husband and no son, this mother's future was not bright. The funeral procession was made up of a large number of residents from Nain. People generally were born, lived, worked, and died in the same town or village for generations. It was likely that most everyone knew this mother and her family and, as was customary, would have participated in this procession.

As the parade of mourners arrived at the gate, so did Jesus. Those that followed him from Capernaum had just witnessed many miracles and probably followed Jesus to see what he would do in Nain. Once again, Jesus was moved by compassion for this widowed mother and said to her, "Weep not" (Lk. 7:13). I don't know if this woman or the residents of Nain knew about Jesus and the many miracles God did through him, but if they did, I'm sure that hope began to take the place of the cries and chants of the mourners as they wept and wailed. Jesus stopped the procession of death and touched the funeral couch on which the deceased lay. He simply said these words to the young man, "I say to you, arise!" (Lk. 7:14 NASB). Immediately, the dead man sat up and began to speak. There is no record of what he said, but he must have joined the chorus of praise expressed by those who had followed Jesus and the residents of the city who now were glorifying God and saying that a great prophet had risen up among them and that God has visited his people. This young man may have been the first-person Jesus raised from the dead. This miracle extended Jesus' fame throughout all of Judea as well as Galilee.

CHAPTER 7

PARABLES OF THE KINGDOM OF GOD

Along the shoreline of the Sea of Galilee and near the city of Capernaum, Jesus entered a fishing boat and sat to teach the multitudes who had gathered there. His parables were stories about the real-life activities of the people of Galilee. Galilee was a rich agricultural region, and the communities that settled around the Sea of Galilee were primarily engaged in farming. Preparing the soil, sowing seeds in their season, protecting the developing plants, and reaping the harvest were daily activities everyone understood. To those with no spiritual understanding, his stories were commonplace and solicited no great appeal or intrigue; however, he was disclosing mysteries hidden in plain sight about how the kingdom of God functions.

Jesus began by telling how a farmer plants seed in the ground. In the process of sowing, some seeds fall on the trampled footpath, and the birds immediately appear to eat the fallen seed. Some of the seed fell on ground that had just a shallow layer of soil on a base of solid rock. It germinated quickly, but because the roots could not penetrate the rock, it soon withered, and the lack of roots to nourish the plant in the scorching sun caused it to die before it could ever develop fruit. Other seeds fell among thorns, and although they sprouted and began to grow, the plants were choked by the multitude of weeds, and they died before they could produce. Lastly, much seed fell on good soil and sprouted, grew to maturity, and developed thirty, sixty, and hundred times more fruit than the single seed that produced the plant. Jesus ended this parable with these instructions, "He that hath ears to hear, let him hear" (Mk. 4:9).

The multitudes left Jesus at this point, or Jesus left the hearers for a more private place because "when he was alone, they that were about him with the twelve asked of him the parable" (Mk. 4:10). Apparently, some who heard this story along with the twelve disciples perceived that there was more to this parable than just a lesson on farming, and those who sought to understand were greatly rewarded.

Before Jesus explained the parable, he reveals to those who came to him that they were the ones who were granted to know the mysteries of the kingdom of God. Those who followed after Jesus and sought to understand the parable were those who had ears to hear. Those that were without, i.e. those who heard only a story on farming, missed the greater spiritual truth Jesus was revealing. These inquirers who received understanding of this parable would have abundance, but those without understanding would have taken from them even the little they had (Mt. 13:12-15). Jesus compared the multitudes to those Isaiah prophesied about, for their hearts were hard, and they have closed their eyes and ears, refusing to hear the truth that would heal them (Mt. 13:14,15; Isa. 6:9).

For those who sought Jesus with eyes that really saw and ears that truly heard were blessed even above the prophets of old who desired to hear the things Jesus was about to reveal.

The Explanation of the Parable

First, Jesus explained the importance of understanding this parable about the seed and the sower. He asked them, if you can't understand the meaning of this parable, how will you understand all the parables? (Mk. 4:13 NLT). This parable then is the foundation for understanding all the parables Jesus told, each explaining how the kingdom of God operates.

Jesus explained that the sower was sowing the word of God. The word of God, like a seed, produces in a person's life just as a seed produces in the soil. Spoken words that are not understood are like seeds that fall on the footpath. Just as the birds steal the seed, so the devil steals the word from those who hear (Mt. 13:19; Mk. 4:15).

Those who hear the word and immediately receive it but have no root to nourish the seed (word) cause it to wither and die. They are like the stony ground. The sun represents the persecution or tribulation that occurs because of the word (seed) the people heard. The word of the kingdom of God is good and desirable. Who does not want to hear that God loves them and has forgiven them of all sin and has delivered them from judgment and made them His sons and daughters, birthing them into His family and giving them His name and authority? No wonder they receive the word with joy (Mt. 13:20). However, just as the scorching sun rises over the tender plant, so trouble comes to the rootless hearer. Persecution for being a follower of Christ or trouble that comes to challenge the word of God is more than the person is willing to endure, and so the promises of that word are never fulfilled. Satan has once again been successful in stopping the fruit of God's kingdom from forming.

The seeds sown among thorns are like those who hear the word of God and receive it, but along with God's word (seed), are sown many other kinds of hurtful and fruitless weed seeds (words). These many distractions and contradictions choke out the life of the seed of God's word. These seeds are described as the cares of this world, the deceitfulness of riches and the lust of other things.

The cares of this world are many. Fears and anxieties often flood the minds of the multitudes. What if this or what if that happens? I'm so afraid; how am I going to pay my bills or overcome this disease? Are my children okay? What if they get hurt or lost or pulled into the wrong crowd? The list is endless, and these weeds must be challenged with the truth of the word of God. In the word of God, the apostle Paul writes, "My God shall supply all your need according to his riches in glory by Christ Jesus (Phil. 4:19). According to Matthew, Jesus "took our infirmities and bare our sickness" in order to fulfill the words of Isaiah the prophet (Mt. 8:17) who said by "his [Christ's] stripes we are healed" (Isa. 53:4,5). Either the word of God will overcome the words of fear, or we will allow words and thoughts of fear to overcome the word of God.

The deceitfulness of riches is another weed to root out of our garden. Riches are not a problem. Riches are actually part of the blessings of God. The love of money (riches) is indeed the root of all evil" (1 Tim. 6:10). "Money is a tool to be used for the purposes of God. "God gives us power to obtain wealth to establish his covenant" (Deut. 8:18), but when money becomes what we love and treasure, that perverted love will place the will of God somewhere further down on our list of important things.

The lust of other things completes the list of weed seeds Jesus mentioned. The weed of lust has to do with our soul, our flesh, and our senses. Lust is an inordinate desire, usually for what is forbidden. Lust of the flesh can be the source of unlawful sexual engagement, gluttony, drunkenness, or other outward performances. But, lust can also be expressed in gossip, criticism, judgments, and unfounded suspicions, as well as pride and arrogance that are sins of the heart. Lust puts the flesh and senses in control instead of the spirit. The apostle Paul notes this truth when he writes, "For to be carnally [fleshly] minded is death, but to be spiritually minded is life and peace (Rom. 8:6 NKJV).

This parable concludes with the purpose of God's word to produce an abundant harvest of increase that is the fruit of the kingdom of God. God's word carries with it the very life of God. The seed that is sown into good ground is the word of God that has a potential of producing a harvest of thirty, sixty and hundred times in increase to what was sown. This is how the kingdom of God works. We hear and understand the word of God (Mt. 13:23). We do not allow Satan to steal it from us through persecution, tribulation, cares of this world, deceitfulness of riches or the lust of other things. We don't allow the distractions of the flesh or afflictions to rob us of the harvest growing within our own hearts or that which we have sown into the lives of others. As we become "rooted and grounded in the love of God" (Eph. 3:17), we will be able to comprehend the things of the Spirit of God and operate in his kingdom because we have had the mysteries that were hidden through the ages revealed to us.

With the conclusion of this parable, Jesus announced to those who heard his explanation that the purpose of a light is to reveal. We would not light a lamp and then hide the light under the bed, but we would place it on the lamp stand in the middle of the room where everyone can benefit from the light. The word of God is a light. Addressing God, the psalmist sings, "Thy word is a lamp unto my feet, and a light unto my path," (119:105). Later, in the same psalm, he adds, "The entrance of [your] words [give] light; it [gives] understanding unto the simple" (Ps. 119:130). The promise Jesus makes to us is that "there is nothing, which shall not be manifested; neither was any thing kept secret, but that it should come abroad" (Mk. 4:22). Again, Jesus reiterates that everyone should listen to him, saying, "If any man have ears to hear, let him hear (Mk. 4:23). If you have the kind of ears to hear and understand the word of God, the mysteries of the kingdom will be revealed to you.

Then Jesus warned those that were listening, saying, "Take heed what you hear" (Mk. 4:24). To take heed is to pay attention, to consider, to see, to discern or to perceive. He added, "For he that hath, to him shall be given: and he that hath not, from him shall be taken even that which he hath" (Mk. 4:25). We must measure the importance of the words we hear and to understand their source and purpose because, if we understand what we hear, more understanding will be given to us. But, if we don't understand what we hear, even what we do understand will be taken from us. We are responsible for not letting the devil steal the word of God out of our hearts. We are to measure its importance and receive it, for it will bring us light and a harvest of good things.

The Parables Continued

Jesus continued to compare the kingdom of God to a seed in several more parables.

In one, he compared the human heart to types of soil, saying, "The kingdom of God is as if a man should cast seed into the ground" (Mk. 4:26). Again, the ground represents the human heart. Once the seed is planted, it continues to grow and mature over the process of time. The farmer sleeps and wakes and waits until the harvest is fully ripe before he harvests the fruit. The important thing for the farmer is to keep the seed in the ground and to be patient until the fruit appears.

Farming is hard work, but once the seed has been planted, the ground will cause the seed to produce the fruit it contains. Getting to the harvest is what we all desire. To see the fruit fully matured and to eat of the harvest and share with others the bounty that has arrived in its season is a joyful time. The process may seem arduous. Dealing with the threats of pests and storms, droughts or floods may be wearisome, but Jesus warned his disciples that this would be the case, saying, "In the world you shall have tribulation" (Jn. 16:33). There are always challenges to the promises and fulfillment of the word of God in our lives, but the word of God never fails. The psalmist declared, "For ever, O Lord, thy word is settled in heaven" (119:89); and the prophet Isaiah, speaking as the mouthpiece of God, proclaimed, "So shall my word be that goes forth out of my mouth: it shall not return unto me void, but it shall accomplish that which I please, and it shall prosper in the thing whereto I sent it" (55:11). As we continue to plant the word of God in our hearts and let the process of growth bring forth "the blade, then the head [of grain], then the mature grain in the head" (Mk. 4:28 AMP) we will be operating in the kingdom of God according to his design.

Jesus' teaching continued with yet another parable about seeds and the kingdom of God. "Whereunto shall we liken the kingdom of God? Or with what comparison shall we compare it? " (Mk. 4:30). Jesus answered his own question by saying, "It is like a grain of mustard seed". The kingdom of God is the greatest of all kingdoms, and Jesus compared his kingdom to the least of all the seeds. The mustard seed is the tiniest seed in the garden. It is an herb that appears in seed form as insignificant. But when this tiny seed is planted, it grows up to become much larger than any of the other herbs in the garden. It literally grows into a small tree, large enough for the birds to safely build their nests in its branches.

Why would Jesus compare the kingdom of God to the least of all the seeds? Many times the things God instructs us to do may seem too simple or even foolish. Naaman was a Syrian general and stood next to the king in authority, but he had a severe problem. He was a leper. Naaman heard that there was a prophet in the land of Israel that could heal him, so he traveled to Samaria and came to house of the prophet Elisha. When he arrived, Elisha sent his servant with a message to Naaman: "Go and wash in the Jordan seven times, and your flesh shall be restored to you, and you shall be clean" (2 Kings 5:10 NKJV). Instead of obeying the voice of God spoken by the prophet, Naaman became angry. He reasoned that the Jordan River was not as clean as some of the rivers in his own country and that dipping seven times in Jordan did not make any sense, and he left in a rage. Some of Naaman's servants who had heard the instructions of the prophet said to Naaman, "…if the prophet had told you to do something great, would you not have done it? How much more then, when he says to you, 'Wash, and be clean'?" (2 Kings. 5:13 NKJV). Naaman then decided to follow the prophet's instructions and went and dipped seven times in the Jordan, and after the seventh time, he came up out of the water, perfectly healed.

What if Naaman had continued in his reasoning that the word of God didn't make any sense? He would have, no doubt, died a leper. But by doing what seemed foolish, he received the fruit of the word of God, and he was healed. We may often think that praying, believing, confessing, giving, loving, and living by the word of God seems foolish, but those simple acts of faith will cause the kingdom of God to grow in our lives until it is greater than anything else. Paul states, "the natural man does not receive the things of the Spirit of God, for they are foolishness to him; nor can he know them, because they are spiritually discerned. But he that is spiritual judges all things…" (1 Cor. 2:14,15 NKJV). Having ears to hear means recognizing the word of God and doing it, knowing that it may seem insignificant, small, and even foolish, but it will prove to be greater than any human reasoning can produce.

Chapter 8

Sailing to the Land of the Gadarenes

After Jesus ended his teaching by parables about the kingdom of God, he said to his disciples, "Let us pass over unto the other side" (Mk. 4:35). He had been teaching near Capernaum on the north end of the lake, and the other side was in reference to the south end in the land known as Gadara. The Sea of Galilee or Lake of Gennesaret was a large fresh water lake about thirteen miles in length. It was late afternoon when they left for Gadara. As they sailed south, they encountered a severe storm of wind. The lake is far below sea level, and the high cliffs surrounding the lake often cause strong winds to circulate on the surface of the water, creating storms of wind without rain. Although this occurrence was common, this wind was not usual. Andrew, Peter, James, and John were all in this boat with Jesus and the other disciples. These men were experienced fishermen who had lived and worked together in a fishing business and had spent many years on these waters, but this time, the winds were so strong they caused the waves to break over the sides of the boat, filling it with water.

Jesus was in the back of the boat asleep even in these stormy conditions. I am sure they refused to awaken him until they became so desperate they saw no other option. What did they expect Jesus to do? Obviously, they did not expect him to do what he did, so their expectations must have been limited to thinking he could provide another pair of hands to help bail water from the sinking boat that was now full. Their method to arouse him from sleep was a cry for help, "Master, do You not care that we are perishing?" (Mk. 4:38 AMPC).

How often, in times of desperation do people in crisis call out to God with these same words, "Don't you care?" Many people have become indifferent or angry at God because they feel like God abandoned them in times of trouble. They may even consider God to be the very source of their trouble, thinking he allowed it or even designed it to teach them some unknown lesson or to punish them for some past transgression. These people have been deceived when they believe that God is somehow against them, that he has total control over the events in the earth and in his sovereignty he either allows or disallows every event that takes place. If that were true, then God would be the author of all the things he has forbidden: murder, rape, genocide, deception, lying, stealing…, and the list goes on. Obviously God does none of these things. Jesus said that in the world we will have tribulation (Jn. 16:33). This is not because he ordained it, but because his kingdom is not of this world. He has nothing to do with the pain and sorrow, the suffering and torment this wayward world produces. On the contrary, he came to heal what was broken and to restore what was stolen by your enemy and his.

The cries of the disciples were met with Jesus standing in the boat and rebuking the wind and the sea with the words, "Peace, be still" (Mk. 4:39). Immediately, the wind ceased and there was a great calm. The disciples must have felt a great relief. Their fear of drowning was over, but suddenly they were overwhelmed by the reality of who Jesus really was and asked each other, "What manner of man is this, that even the wind and the sea obey him?" (Mk. 4:41). Mark's record says, "they feared exceedingly" (Mk. 4:41) because of the power and authority Jesus demonstrated when he spoke to the wind, but they were totally unprepared for Jesus' rebuke: "Why are [you] so fearful? How is it that [you] have no faith?" (Mk. 4:40). Could Jesus be implying that they somehow had the authority to do what he did—that they could have rebuked the wind instead of bailed the water? I believe Jesus was preparing them for the days to come when he would send them out two by two to "heal the sick, cleanse the lepers, raise the dead, cast out demons" and preach the gospel (Mt. 10:7,8). Moving mountains and cursing fig trees were all examples Jesus used to show us that he is the one with all authority in heaven and in earth and he has given us his name of go and do the same things he did and even greater things because the Spirit of God has come to empower his church to believe the impossible and do the miraculous (Jn. 14:12-14).

The Land of Gadara

The land of the Gadarenes was on the south end of the Sea of Galilee. Jesus and the twelve disciples probably arrived there at night after leaving the north end of the lake in the evening and then encountering the storm a few hours later. Having calmed the wind and waves, Jesus and the disciples should have arrived before midnight but may have remained in the boat until sunup. Whatever the hour, one thing is clear. When Jesus stepped out of the boat, immediately there met him a man* who was so hostile and dangerous ("exceedingly fierce" Mt. 8:28) that nobody would go near that area (Mt. 8:28; Mk. 5:1; Lk. 8:26).

This man was so filled and controlled by demonic spirits that he terrorized the whole community. Even when the people apprehended him and bound him with chains, his possession gave him super-human strength that broke the chains. He lived in the tombs with the dead, wore no clothes, and his torment was revealed by his constant loud cries which were heard day and night as he cut himself with sharp stones. As powerful as this possession was to control the actions of this man who "was driven of the devil" (Lk. 8:29), all the forces of the wicked could not keep him from worshipping Jesus when he saw him, for he fell at his feet and "worshipped him" (Mk. 5:6).

Suddenly, fearful voices cried out of this man, "What have I to do with [you], Jesus, Son of the most high God? I adjure [you] by God, that [you] torment me not" (Mk. 5:7). The cries of desperation were the result of the command by Jesus for the spirits to "Come out of the man" (Mk. 5:8). The words were not from this man, but from the many unclean spirits that inhabited his body.

In another place Jesus taught about unclean spirits, saying, "When an unclean spirit goes out of a man, he goes through dry places, seeking rest, and finds none. Then he says, 'I will return to my house from which I came.' And when he is come, he finds it empty…Then he goes and takes with him seven other spirits more wicked than himself, and they enter and dwell there…" (Mt. 12:43-45 NKJV). Here Jesus shows us that more than one unclean spirit can live in the body of a person at a time. Jesus mentioned eight spirits inhabiting the body of a man besides the man's own human spirit. Since a spirit

---

*Both Mark's account and Luke's account of this story state that a possessed man met Jesus. When discussing the same story, Matthew writes that two demon-possessed men met Jesus. This difference may exist because Matthew's account correctly reveals that there were two men, while Mark and Luke just focus on the one man that was better known in the region, and Jesus' interaction with him was dominate.

is non-corporal, he does not take up space. Therefore, an indefinite number can cohabit together in a single body.

After his initial command, Jesus asked, "What is your name?" (Mk. 5:9), And the man replied, "My name is Legion: for we are many" (Mk. 5:9). Jesus was not asking the man his name but the possessing spirits that controlled him. The name given was Legion, and the reason they called themselves by that name was that they were "many". The term legion in that day was typically referencing a Roman legion of soldiers. The size of a legion varied widely depending on the times and region of the empire, but a Roman legion was typically described as having between 2,000 and 6,000 soldiers. Does this mean that this many unclean spirits inhabited the man? No, but it is interesting that the spirits that left the man entered into a herd of about 2,000 pigs (Mk.5:13). Regardless of the exact number, we know there were many spirits that lived in the body of this man.

One thing you do not see here is a cosmic battle or intense struggle between Jesus and the many unclean spirits he encountered. Sometimes the idea is presented that the struggle between God and the Devil is an endless wrestling match where sometimes God prevails and sometimes the Devil does, but this is not what we see in the scriptures. Anytime Jesus comes up against an unclean spirit, he simply cast it out. He didn't break a sweat or strain a muscle to bring deliverance to the oppressed. Actually, in the many scriptural examples of Jesus entering the presence of one with an unclean spirit, we see the shear terror of those spirits as they beg Jesus not to "torment [them] before the time" (Mt. 8:29). There was never a question of if these foul spirits would be cast out. The only question was under what terms they should leave. In the case of the Legion, the spirits begged Jesus greatly not to "send them away out of the country" (Mk. 5:10). Apparently, these spirits had an easier influence in this region because of the large Gentile population. Pigs were considered an unclean animal, and no orthodox Jewish community would tolerate the raising of swine in their district.

The compassion of Jesus for this man, who ran and worshipped him even in his desperate and tormented condition, must have been great. The needs of this man far exceeded the economic profitability of the herd, and so Jesus allowed the spirits to enter the swine. The devil was trying to make the most of his untenable situation and likely sought to discover a way to turn this community against Jesus. If Jesus had been blamed for the financial loss, then the people would have rejected him without hearing what he had to say. It seems that this plan must have succeeded to some degree, for those who fed the swine went and told the people in the country and in the city that the whole herd ran off the cliff and perished in the waters of the lake. The entire community came to see what happened and found Jesus and the man who had terrorized them, but instead of being naked and crazed, he was clothed and "in his right mind" (Mk. 5:15). Their awe and wonder were quickly traded for fear and uncertainty, and instead of rejoicing in the man's deliverance, they begged Jesus to leave their coasts. As Jesus was entering the boat, the formerly demonized man begged Jesus to take him with him and the other disciples, but Jesus sent the man home to tell his family of the wonderful things the Lord had done for him. As always, Jesus' love and compassion overcame the tactics and devices of the devil, for this man not only told his family, but he also traveled throughout the Decapolis telling everyone what Jesus had done for him. Although Jesus was rejected in Gadara, his mission was successful. He had delivered a man from his tormentors, a community from danger, and this man's testimony reached the people of ten cities instead of just the hill country south of the lake.

Chapter 9

Jairus, a Ruler of the Synagogue

The people of the city of Capernaum must have been watching for Jesus, for when he returned from Gadara, a multitude had gathered and were waiting for him (Mk. 5:21). Jesus was still near the shoreline when the ruler of the synagogue broke through the crowd to get to Jesus.

Jairus was a ruler of the synagogue in Capernaum, a very important man in the city, and well known to everyone. He was likely one of the delegates who went to Jesus on behalf of the Roman centurion. Jairus may also have witnessed the healing of the paralyzed man lowered through the roof to Jesus. In addition, he may have been present on the Sabbath day when Jesus healed the man with the crippled hand. He may have been one of those rulers who even sought the Herodians to destroy Jesus or been a party to those who considered Jesus' words of forgiveness as blasphemous, but now he was in a crisis. His twelve-year-old daughter was dying, and like most fathers, he was willing to seek help for her, whatever the cost. Having witnessed many miracles by the hands of Jesus, Jairus was now desperate to get to him. As he burst through the crowds along the seashore, he fell before Jesus, not caring about the perceptions of the people. He begged for Jesus' help. If only Jesus would come with him to his house and would lay his hands on his daughter, she would be healed (Mk. 5:23).

Jesus could have scolded Jairus for his open opposition to him, but Jesus was not like other men who only considered the outward appearance. Instead, he looked into the heart of this man, and being moved with compassion, he went with him. God is slow to anger and of great mercy; he opposes the proud but "gives grace to the humble" (James 4:6). Jesus represented perfectly the character and nature of his Father as this proud man humbled himself before Jesus seeking help for his only daughter (Lk. 8:42).

As Jesus walked with Jairus, many people gathered around them and went with them. This crowd is described as a "throng" that "pressed upon him". This multitude crowded the busy streets of Capernaum on the way to Jairus' house. A "certain woman" (Mk. 5:25) which had an issue of blood for twelve years made her way through the crowd of people to get close enough to Jesus to touch the hem of his garment.

This woman was desperate to get to Jesus, and even in her weakened condition, pushed her way through the crowd to touch his garment. Matthew's account says she touched the hem of his garment (Mt. 9:20). Luke records her touching the border of his garment (Lk. 8:44), while Mark just says she touched his garment, saying within herself, "If I may touch but his clothes, I shall be whole" (Mk. 5:28).

Some have suggested that Jesus wore the typical clothing of the rabbis, which included a blue ribbon running along the hem of the outer robe. This was worn because God had instructed Moses to tell the children of Israel to "make them fringes in the borders of their garments ...and put upon the fringe of the borders a ribbon of blue" (Num. 15:38). This ribbon of blue was to remind Israel of the commandments and promises of the covenant. By touching the blue ribbon on the fringe of Jesus' garment, this woman was grabbing hold of the promise of God for her healing.

Whether or not Jesus wore the ribbon of blue, this woman was making a very bold demonstration of her faith. A woman, in her physical condition, was banned from being in a crowd of people because she was considered unclean and would make anyone she touched unclean. If she was caught being in a crowd, she could have been severely punished, and the very person who could enforce the judgment against her stood right next to Jesus, the ruler of the synagogue. This woman's determination and great faith led her to press through the crowd to get to Jesus, whatever the cost. When she touched his clothes, she immediately felt in her body, that she had been healed (Mk. 5:29). At the same time, Jesus felt power leave his body, and he turned around and said to his disciples, "Who touched my clothes?" The disciples replied, "You see the multitude thronging you, and you say, 'Who touched me?'" In other words, his disciples were amazed that Jesus would ask such a question because of the large number of people, and many of whom were touching him. However, it was not the physical touch of the people that Jesus questioned; it was the touch of faith that drew from the anointing upon him. As he looked at the multitude, he saw a woman who trembled in his presence. Knowing she could not stay hidden, she came and "fell down before him, and told him all the truth" (Mk. 5:33). In telling Jesus "all the truth" she must have given a detailed accounting of the past twelve years of suffering. She had, "suffered many things of many physicians, and had spent all that she had, and was no better, but rather grew worse" (Mk. 5:26 NKJV).

The Talmud, which is a collection of Jewish laws, civil and religious, as well as rabbinical teaching, includes eleven possible cures for a woman suffering from chronic menstrual bleeding. Modern medicine identify six tonics or astringents that may have been beneficial to this woman, but the other five were based merely on superstition and would have added only humiliation to her suffering. According to Alfred Edersheim (page 426, "The Life and Times of Jesus The Messiah") these superstitions included obtaining the ashes of an ostrich egg carried in a linen or cotton cloth or finding in barleycorn in the dung of a white female donkey.

At the conclusion of this woman's testimony Jesus said to her, "Daughter, your faith has made you whole; go in peace, and be whole of your plague" (Mk. 5:34). Jesus never seemed to be in a hurry as he patiently listened to this thankful woman. However, Jairus was not likely pleased with the delay this woman caused. After all, his little girl was dying, and getting Jesus to her bedside was his only concern. As Jesus concluded his conversation with this woman, a messenger arrived with sad news for Jairus, announcing, "Your daughter is dead" (Mk. 5:35). Upon hearing this, Jesus said to the ruler of the synagogue, "Be not afraid, only believe." Jesus sent the crowd away, allowing no one to follow him except Peter, James, and John. These three only accompanied him to Jairus' house. The turmoil at the house included the professional mourners who had already arrived upon hearing of the death of the ruler's daughter.

It was customary to express grief with loud wails and cries of sorrow for the dead. The wealthy would hire professional mourners to "weep and wail, greatly" (Mk. 5:38), enhancing the true sorrow expressed by the family. When Jesus arrived, he addressed these mourners by saying, "Why make this ado, and weep? The damsel is not dead, but sleeps" (Mk. 5:39). Their scornful laughter at Jesus' comments was quickly dismissed as Jesus "put them all out" (Mk. 5:40). Jesus always seized control of the situation. He took the young girl's father and mother and the disciples that came with him into the bedroom where she lay. Taking her by the hand, Jesus said, "Damsel, I say unto [you], arise." And she "arose and walked" (Mk. 5:41,42). Those that witnessed this miracle were "astonished with a great astonishment," but Jesus commanded them to tell no one and to give the girl something to eat. The miraculous works of Jesus were often coupled with the practical needs of those to whom he ministered. The girl may have been sick for days and greatly dehydrated, eating or drinking would be necessary for her to regain her strength.

Why would Jesus not want this family to tell everyone about how he raised this girl from the dead? The true reason may not be known, but out of all the many hundreds of people Jesus healed, only three were raised from the dead. The widow's son at Nain, Lazarus, and this girl are the only ones that are recorded in the scriptures. There could have been many others because of John's statement about the books that could have been written if everything Jesus did had been recorded, "even the world itself could not contain the books that should be written" (Jn. 21:25). But these are the three that are specifically recorded, and in them, we see the love and compassion of God for a grieving widow over her only son, Lazarus, a personal friend of Jesus, and the daughter of the synagogue ruler. Wouldn't it be fascinating to know what these three individuals accomplished in the years that followed their rising from the dead?

CHAPTER 10

JESUS IN JERUSALEM AT BETHESDA

There are many places whose names begin with "Beth" which means "house of." Bethabara is "House of passage," Bethphage is "House of figs," Bethany is "House of dates," and Bethesda is "House of mercy." Bethesda was in the city of Jerusalem at the entrance of the "Sheep gate" where there was a pool surrounded by five porches. The porches were made to house the many sick, crippled, and infirmed that came to the pool, hoping to be healed of whatever disease that plagued them for an angel would come at a certain time and trouble or stir the waters of the pool. The first person that stepped into the water after the angel touched the waters would be healed of their infirmity (Jn. 5:1-4).

I am amazed at how many commentators and scholars have dissected this passage to try to and explain what "really" happened. Everything from minor earthquakes to the pool being an artisan well that would simply bubble up on occasion and cause the superstitious observers to step into the water and then believe that they were healed because of some psychosomatic episode is used to explain away what the Bible declares. Why not just believe that an angel would stir the waters of the pool that brought real healing to the first one who touched the water? Too often people want to explain away the work of the miraculous because they don't understand the how or why. Why the angel would do what he did or how that action caused the water to bring healing to the afflicted does not need to be explained, only believed. Obviously, the five porches, filled with the sick, should be evidence enough that these healings were legitimate. Otherwise, the people would not continue to gather at the House of Mercy.

Jesus arrived in Jerusalem with the many joyful worshippers to celebrate the Feast of Passover. Jesus chose to enter the city through the "Sheep Gate" which was customarily used to bring the sacrificial animals to the Temple. The "Lamb of God" would enter these gates the following year and be inspected at the Temple and then sacrificed on the cross. As Isaiah declared, "But he was wounded for our transgressions, he was bruised for our iniquities: the chastisement of our peace was upon him; and with his stripes we are healed" (Isa. 53:5).

The hopeful multitude was focused on the waters of the pool when Jesus arrived. His attention was immediately drawn to a man which had an infirmity for thirty-eight years and had come to the pool, hoping to be healed (Jn. 5:5). As he approached the man, Jesus asked him this question, "[Will you] be made whole?" (Jn. 5:6). This question may suggest one of two things, "Do you think you will be healed?" or "Do you want to be healed?" The man's response reveals his frustration; "I have no man, to put me …into the pool" (Jn. 5:7). His desire was to be made whole, but he had no real hope of that happening without someone to help him. As the man lay on his makeshift bed among so many others, Jesus said to him, "Rise, take up your bed, and walk" (Jn. 5:8). The man was immediately made whole and did as Jesus instructed him. He picked up his bed and left the place of the infirmed joining the many worshippers going to the Temple (Jn. 5:9).

There is no record of this man thanking Jesus or praising God for his miraculous recovery. We only know that he picked up his bed and left. When questioned by the Jewish leadership about why he was violating the laws of the Sabbath day for carrying his bed, the man told them, "He that made me whole, the same said unto me, Take up your bed, and walk" (Jn. 5:11). He acknowledged that a man had healed him, but when the Jews asked what the man's name was, he did not know. Apparently, this man was accompanied by some of the Jewish leaders to the pool to find out who had told him to carry his bed. It is interesting that they were more concerned about the violation of the law and seeking judgment against this unknown healer than they were amazed that a man who had suffered so much had been made whole after thirty-eight years of sickness.

By the time they returned, Jesus had left the multitude still gathered around the pool. The scriptures do not reveal the threats the religious leaders must have made against this man, but in the following verses, we find Jesus in the Temple, seeking this same man and saying to him, "Behold you are made whole: sin no more, lest a worse thing come upon you" (Jn. 5:14). In this man's case, was some sin the reason for his years of suffering, or was Jesus warning him of the Jewish leaders' perception that he sinned by violating the Sabbath day and would be judged accordingly? Their intent was to "slay" Jesus for healing the man and telling him to carry his bed on the Sabbath day, for when this man knew it was Jesus who had healed him, he immediately went to the Jewish council and told them (Jn. 5:15,16). Was Jesus delivering the man from both sickness and the judgment of this capital offense the Jews accused him of? If the Jews sought to slay Jesus for violating the Sabbath would they not also desire to slay the man for carrying his bed, which would carry the same judgment? Maybe that is why this man was so quick to run to the council and report that Jesus was the healer they were looking for.

CHAPTER 11

JESUS FEEDING THE 5,000

After leaving Jerusalem, Jesus returned to Galilee, teaching in the synagogues and healing the multitudes that followed him. Nearly a year later, we find Jesus on the banks of the Sea of Galilee with his disciples. He had sent them out two by two into the towns and villages of Galilee, healing the sick, casting out demons, and preaching the gospel (Mk. 6:7-13; Lk. 9:6). They returned to Jesus exhausted from their journey but excited about what God had done through them as they ministered to the people by the anointing Jesus had given them. They found little time to rest as many people seeking help were constantly coming and going. Jesus told them to come with him as he entered a boat and journeyed southward toward the city of Tiberias on the central west side of the lake. As they sailed, many people recognized them and followed the boat along the shoreline. By the time they arrived at their destination, there was a multitude of people waiting for them. Jesus, being moved by compassion, sat down and began to teach the multitudes. By the end of that day, his disciples encouraged him to send the crowds away to buy food for themselves. Jesus responded by asking Philip, "Where shall we buy bread, that these may eat?" (Jn. 6:5). Philip told Jesus that what they had was not sufficient to buy enough bread for them all to eat. Andrew, overhead the conversation and surveying what was available said to Jesus, "there is a lad here, which has five barley loaves and two small fishes," but he quickly realized how insignificant that information sounded and said, probably under his breath, "but what are they among so many?"

With that Jesus told his disciples to have all the people sit down in groups of 100's and 50's while he took the 5 biscuit sized barley loaves and the two sardine-like fish and blessed them. Jesus must have had each disciple bring a basket for him to fill with the fish and bread to distribute to the many groups that covered the hillside. They all ate until they were filled, and the disciples brought the baskets with the remaining fragments back to him (Jn. 6:10-13). I imagine that Jesus returned the young boy's loaves and fish, which were now contained in the 12 baskets filled with what remained of this miracle meal.

This must be a very important story, for it is the only one that is recorded in all four gospels. In these few verses, we find the heart of God. Here, Jesus and the twelve were trying to "get away," take a break from the busy ministry schedule. They had no rest, not even time enough to eat because of the demands of the people. They were on their way to a well-deserved rest, which they intended to enjoy, but as they arrived, Jesus saw the multitudes and was moved with compassion for them. Instead of seeking some other location or chasing away the crowd, he sat down and began to teach them. Maybe some of the teaching we read about in other places is what Jesus was teaching this group. He may have ministered to them out of his own need. His words explained what his actions illustrated: the value of laying down our lives for someone else instead of saving ourselves (for our own comfort and convenience) to give to those in need.

This miracle also challenges the old saying that "God will give you what you need, not what you want." There was no real need for Jesus to feed these five thousand men plus the women and children who were there. They would not have died of hunger if they had not experienced this miracle, but Jesus wanted to feed them. He wanted to bless them and show them the love of God.

The young boy who came that day with his own lunch must have been willing to give Jesus what he had. In return, he got his lunch back and twelve baskets more. Jesus said, "Give and it shall be given to you good measure, pressed down and shaken together and running over" (Lk. 6:38). That was made abundantly obvious as this young boy carried home much more than he had when he arrived. Sowing and reaping, giving and receiving activate spiritual laws of increase just as sowing a field produces a harvest of fruit in its season.

Walking on Water

After feeding the multitudes, Jesus sent his disciples ahead of him to the city of Bethsaida on the other side of the lake. After they had departed in the boat, Jesus sent the people away and went up to a high place overlooking the Sea of Galilee. There he prayed until the fourth watch of the night which is from 3:00 AM to 6:00 AM. The Gospel of Mark records that, from his place of prayer, Jesus saw the disciples "toiling in rowing" because the wind was against them. Apparently, this was not a rainstorm but one of the usual windstorms created by the unique orientation of the lake, and facing into the wind, those in the boat found it difficult to make much headway as they rowed. Maybe it was a moonlit night, and Jesus could see the men in the boat from miles away, or maybe he saw a vision of them by the Spirit as he was praying. Either way, he recognized their struggle.

The question we need to ask is "Why were the disciples on the lake at that time of night in the first place?" The scriptures reveal that Jesus had decided to feed the multitudes near the end of the previous day. No indication is given about how much time it took to distribute the bread and the fish to the potential seven or ten or more thousands of people (5,000 men plus women and children) that had gathered. After the disciples finished serving the people, Jesus told them to get in the boat and go to the other side of the lake which was probably about six or seven miles. They must have arrived on the shore of Bethsaida an hour or so later. Could it be that an hour's journey took them some nine to twelve hours to complete or did something else happen?

If we consider all three of the gospels that record this story, we find in John's gospel that "when evening came, His disciples went down to the sea, got into the boat, and went over the sea toward Capernaum. And it was already dark, and Jesus had not come to them" (Jn. 6:16,17 NKJV). Why were they going to Capernaum when Jesus told them to go to Bethsaida? It would seem that Jesus sent them to Bethsaida ahead of him and he was going to come and join them there. So we can assume that they went to Bethsaida to wait for Jesus, but when he did not show up as quickly as they had expected and it was getting dark, they got back into the boat to go to Capernaum where Jesus was living. It was during this journey to Capernaum that they found themselves "toiling in rowing because the wind was against them." If they had just done what Jesus told them to do, they would not have gotten caught in the storm of wind. How often does impatience get us into trouble as it did Jesus' disciples? We hear from God and think things should happen immediately, and when they don't, our impatience causes us to make rash decisions that bring us needlessly into trouble.

We read that from his place of prayer Jesus saw the disciples struggling in the wind and he went to them. Many have believed that he was going to their rescue but that is not what happened. Mark's gospel tells us that when Jesus came to them "he would have passed by them" (Mk. 6:48). Jesus was going to the place where he had told them to go which was Bethsaida.

I'm sure the disciples were expecting Jesus to arrive by boat like they did, but instead Jesus is walking on the water. This unusual sight caused them to scream aloud in fear, believing they were seeing a ghost crossing the water in the wind. Jesus assured them that it was he that was walking on the water and not some phantom. Matthew's gospel gives us further insight into that night's events because Peter spoke up and said to Jesus "Lord, if it is You, bid me come unto you on the water" (Mt. 14:28 MEV,). Was Peter testing this figure walking on the water to confirm that it really was Jesus? Was he really expecting Jesus to tell him to come and walk on the water with him? "Come" was the only response Jesus had to Peter's request. Upon that word, Peter stepped over the side of the boat and began walking on the water, going to Jesus. It seems that Peter was doing fine until he began looking at the wind and the waves. The circumstances began to override his temporary demonstration of faith, and he began to fear and sink into the water. Calling upon Jesus to save him brought Jesus' immediate response to stretch out his hand and catch Peter. With the help of Jesus, Peter walked with him on the water back to the boat. This remarkable experience was worth the retort Jesus gave Peter, "O you of little faith, why did you doubt?" (Mt. 14:31 NKJV). Faith in the single word command Jesus gave "Come" caused Peter to experience something none of the other disciples did. Peter walked on water. Here, again is one of those times when there was no life and death situation that required Peter to experience this miracle of walking on water. He just wanted to walk on water, and Jesus gave him the desire of his heart.

Another miracle associated with this same event is only mentioned in John's gospel. Here we are told that, as soon as Jesus got into the boat with the disciples, the boat was immediately transported to the "land where they were going" (Jn. 6:21). The other gospels say that the wind immediately ceased, a miracle we have seen before when the boat was being swamped in the storm (Mk. 4:39). But John reveals that the boat and all aboard were transported from somewhere between Bethsaida and Capernaum on the Sea of Galilee to the land of Gennesaret.

This supernatural transport is seen one other time in scripture when Philip was baptizing the Ethiopian eunuch, and as soon as the eunuch came out of the water "the Spirit of the Lord caught away Philip, that the eunuch saw him no more" (Acts 8:39). The next verse says that Philip was found at Azotus, a city about twenty miles from where Philip had baptized the eunuch.

This account of Jesus walking on the water concludes with the boat and all of the disciples supernaturally transported to the land of Gennesaret. The Sea of Galilee is also referred to as Lake Gennesaret, so the land of Gennesaret may just give reference to the fact that they were on the water but were suddenly on the land. A level plain between Capernaum and Bethsaida may have been the location of their arrival. When Jesus and the disciples got out of the boat, the people "knew him" (Mk. 6:54). They began running through the entire region, telling everyone that Jesus had come, and with that news, the people began bringing the sick in their beds to wherever they heard Jesus was. Mark's gospel records that Jesus traveled throughout that region, entering into villages, cities, and even the more rural areas, and wherever he went, they brought the sick in beds and laid them in the streets where Jesus walked, only desiring to touch the border of his garment "and as many as touched him were made whole" (Mk. 6:56).

Can you visualize what was taking place here? Someone saw that Jesus was about to enter a town and ran ahead of him, announcing to everyone that Jesus was coming. The people of the town immediately brought their sick and laid them in the street as Jesus was approaching them. They requested that he simply walk close enough to them that they could reach out and touch the border of his garment, and all those who touched it were immediately made well. In front of Jesus, was a large number of sick and crippled people, lying in the street, waiting to touch him. As they were healed, they began following Jesus with ecstatic praise. A sea of suffering before him was replaced with a multitude of healed and whole people, giving to God an anthem of praise as they followed the one who healed them. Just as the woman with the issue of blood may have touched the ribbon of blue in the fringe of Jesus' garment, so those who made up this multitude of suffering took hold of the promises of God by faith in the one who came in the name of the Father to show forth his glory.

The Bread of Life

Prior to his journey throughout the towns and villages of Gennesaret, Jesus had miraculously arrived in the boat with his disciples the day after he had fed the multitude with the bread and fish. Some of those who had eaten the day before from this miraculous provision were again looking for Jesus. They had made their way to Capernaum where they found Jesus and his disciples. Their question to him was, "Rabbi, when did you come here"? (Jn. 6:25 NKJV). Instead of answering their question, he addressed the real reason they came looking for him. "You seek me, not because you saw the miracles, but because you ate of the loaves, and were filled" (Jn. 6:26 NKJV). In other words, they were looking for another free meal. Jesus instructed them to not seek after perishable food i.e. a temporary provision, but to seek the kind of food that will endure to everlasting life. They were laboring to find Jesus, but they were looking for the temporary when Jesus wanted to give them the eternal.

These seekers were like most multitudes that came to Jesus. They were locked into the natural, physical realm where their daily needs were the focus of their labor. When Jesus instructed them not to work for the food that quickly perishes but to seek that which is eternal, they replied, "What shall we do, that we might work the works of God?" (Jn. 6:28). The work of God, Jesus said, was to believe in him. Immediately, the crowd demanded a sign from Jesus so they might believe, and they did not want just any sign but a sign that would do for them what Moses did for Israel in the wilderness. They wanted daily manna provided for them. Again, the crowd was seeking something to eat.

As the crowd demanded the bread of heaven, Jesus again brought their attention to the eternal, "Moses gave you not that bread from heaven; but my Father gives you the true bread from heaven. For the bread of God is He who comes down from heaven and gives life unto the world" (Jn. 6:32,33 NKJV). With visions of unending provision, the people again demanded, "…give us this bread…" (Jn. 6:34).

The remainder of this chapter records Jesus' attempt to teach them about the bread of heaven. The Jews constantly challenged his origin and purpose, for they knew only of his earthly origin, sighting Joseph and Mary as his parents and Galilee as his country. They refused to believe he came down from heaven or that God was his Father, and when Jesus suggested that eternal life was available only if they would eat his flesh and drink his blood (Jn. 6:53,54), many of them left him and "walked no more with him" (Jn. 6:66). Eating unclean flesh and drinking blood was an abomination to Jewish ears. They could not imagine that this miracle worker was suggesting such a thing. Turning to the twelve, Jesus said, "Will you also go away?" (Jn. 6:67 AMPC). Peter quickly answered for the twelve, "Lord, to whom shall we go? You have the words of eternal life. And we …believe and are sure that You are that Christ, the Son of the living God" (Jn. 6:68,69 NKJV).

How often had Peter and the twelve been confused by the things Jesus said applying his words as literal actions, missing the spiritual meaning Jesus intended? This time Peter better understood that the words of Jesus were, "spirit, and life" (Jn. 6:63).

The bread of life discourse ended Jesus' Galilean ministry. He would spend the next year slowly making his way through the region of Perea toward Jerusalem, the Temple, and the cross.

CHAPTER 12

Jesus' Perean Ministry

Jesus' final year of ministry is known as the Perean ministry. As he left the region of Galilee, he began his final trip toward Jerusalem, making his way along the eastside of the Jordan valley, passing through the land of Perea although he had intended to return to Samaria first. Luke writes, "Now it came to pass, when the time had come for Him to be received up, that He steadfastly set His face to go to Jerusalem, and sent messengers before His face. And as they went, they entered a village of the Samaritans, to prepare for Him. But they did not receive Him, because His face was *set* for the journey to Jerusalem" (Lk. 9:51-53 NKJV). Jesus had sent messengers into the Samaritan village to make arrangements for him and his disciples.

We are not told who these messengers were, but when they returned to Jesus and the disciples, they informed them that the Samaritans would not allow Jesus to enter their village. James and John responded to the news saying, "Lord, do you want us to call fire down from heaven to destroy these people?" (Lk. 9:54 CEV). These words indicate that the old rivalry between the Jews and the Samaritans was alive and well. The prejudices of the Samaritans would prohibit them from receiving the miraculous works and the words of life Jesus had intended to bring them, and the response of James and John revealed their disdain for the Samaritan people. In their zeal to defend Jesus, they unknowingly had given place to the wrong spirit. "You do not know what kind of spirit you are of; for the Son of Man did not come to destroy men's lives, but to save them." (Lk. 9:55,56 NASB). Jesus did not rebuke James and John for their boastful statement, equating themselves with the prophet Elijah, but he did reveal to them that their purpose to destroy those who rejected him was not the will of God. His purpose was to save, not to destroy, and any spiritual motivation outside of that purpose was not of God. Passing by Samaria they continued their journey to Perea.

Jesus Sending out the Seventy

There is no record of the number of those who called themselves disciples of Jesus. We know that, from the many disciples who followed him, Jesus he had chosen the twelve whom he called apostles (Lk. 6:13). Now, in the regions of Perea, he chose seventy disciples and sent them ahead of him into the cities and villages. Giving them very specific instructions of what to take and what not to take with them, he sent them out by twos and directed them to heal the sick and declare the kingdom of God to all who would listen. They were to stay with those who received them, but publicly shake off the dust of the towns that refused them (Lk. 10:1-11).

The works these seventy accomplished must have been significant because Jesus said the most notoriously wicked cities in history would have repented had they seen these mighty works. Therefore, he added, the judgment on those who had seen and not believed would be devastating. Then, Jesus began to list by name the cities where he had worked so many miracles, and still they rejected him (Lk. 10:12-16).

Having accomplished the mission the seventy returned with great joy to report what had happened. They said to Jesus, "Lord, even the demons are subject to us in your name" (Lk. 10:17 AMP). Jesus immediately responded with, "I beheld Satan as lightning fall from heaven."

The strongholds of wicked spirits that governed people's lives were being cast down from their exalted position as these seventy believers went to the people with the power and authority of the name of Jesus, the one who had commissioned them, saying, "Behold, I give unto you authority to tread on serpents and scorpions, and over all the power of the enemy: and nothing shall by any means hurt you" (Lk. 10:19). Remember, these were not the twelve apostles or some elite spiritual group that walked in great wisdom and maturity, but these were those whom Jesus described as not wise or prudent but "babes" (Lk. 10:21). These were those who simply received what Jesus gave them and then obeyed his command to go. I'm sure they would not have been deemed qualified by the religious leaders of their day, for they were not educated in their universities or credentialed by their organizations. Judged unqualified and ignorant as Peter and John would later be called (Acts 4:13), these "babes" performed the miraculous and began the dismantling of Satan's kingdom.

After Jesus directed them to rejoice most of all because their names are written in heaven, he then rejoiced. This word *rejoiced* literally means to jump up and spin around with joy. What an expression of the delight by Jesus when he saw in these seventy the future of his church and the transforming work that would be accomplished through the gospel. They were about to enter into a new age that prophets and kings of the past had longed to see. But that time had not yet come because Jesus had not yet been glorified, and so had not sent the Spirit upon all who believed (Jn. 7:39).

THE GOOD SAMARITAN

In Perea, Jesus is confronted by a lawyer. The scriptures do not identify where Jesus had this conversation with this one who was considered an expert in the Law of Moses, but most likely, it was in one of the synagogues, for this man "stood up" (Lk. 10:25) to tempt Jesus. The scribes, Pharisees, rulers of the synagogues, and doctors of the Law often tried to entrap Jesus as he taught the people. Apparently, this was another time where they tried to find a way to accuse and condemn him. This lawyer asks Jesus, "Master, what shall I do to inherit eternal life?" (Lk.10:25). Although this man's question may sound like a sincere desire to better understand what Jesus was teaching, his actions and purposes are revealed to us by Luke. He "stood up," not in honor of Jesus, but with the purpose of intimidating him and discrediting him by his answer. Jesus was well aware of his intent, and instead of answering him, Jesus asked him to answer his own question, "What is written in the law? How do you read it?" (Lk. 10:26 AMP). After all, this man was an expert in the law and certainly should have known what the law said. The lawyer answered correctly, "'You shall love the Lord your God with all your heart, and with all your soul, and with all your strength, and with all your mind,' and 'your neighbor as yourself'" (Lk. 10:27 NKJV). By answering his own question and having Jesus agree with his answer, Jesus successfully avoided the lawyer's evil purpose. Trying again to find some way of accusing Jesus, the lawyer asked him another question, "And who is my neighbor?" (Lk. 10:29). Jesus answered by telling a story to all who were present.

This story of the Good Samaritan describes three men who had an opportunity to be a good neighbor to a victim of a brutal beating and robbery. This poor man was lying in the road, bleeding and half dead. The first to arrive on the scene was a priest who should have shown mercy to this man, but instead crossed the street to avoid going near him. The second man to arrive at this crime scene was a Levite. Like the priest, he would have been expected to show mercy to this man in need. After all, the Levites were those who fulfilled the Law of Moses by ministering to God in the Temple, but the Levite also passed by this man without helping him. The third man to pass that way was a Samaritan. Hated by the priests, Levites, and lawyers, this man went to the one in need and showed him compassion by binding up his wounds and carrying him on his donkey to an inn where he took care of him and even paid the inn keeper to continue meeting this man's needs until he had fully recovered. Finishing this story, Jesus turns to the lawyer and asks him which one of these three was a neighbor to the man in need?

Not only did Jesus avoid saying anything the lawyer could legally use against him, he put the lawyer on the spot by asking him, once again, to answer his own question. "Who is my neighbor?" The lawyer had no choice; "He that showed mercy" (Lk. 10:37) was the good neighbor to the man in need and thus fulfilled the word of God.

The actions of the priest and the Levite in the story Jesus told would have been acceptable according to the teaching of the religious leaders. Those who were sick, diseased, robbed, or beaten were believed to be under the judgment of God for some sin they or their parents had committed, and the priest or Levite would have interfered with God's justice if they tried to help.

This erroneous teaching created a mindset that was commonly believed and one Jesus had to constantly challenge. When Jesus encountered the man who had been born blind, his own disciples questioned him about whose sin caused the blindness "this man, or his parents?" (Jn. 9:2). Jesus' answer to them was neither the blind man or his parents had sinned to cause his blindness. The rejection and judgment felt by so many suffering with leprosy, lameness, blindness, or any kind of misfortune touched the heart of Jesus, who "went about doing good, and healing all that were oppressed of the devil; for God was with him" (Acts. 10:38). While sin opened the door of oppression to all of humanity, those who were suffering did not need the judgment and contempt offered by the religious community. They needed the revelation of God's goodness and mercy and help like the Samaritan gave the man in need. Jesus did "not come to destroy men's lives, but to save them" (Lk. 9:56). This Samaritan, who was looked down on by the orthodox community was the one who best represented the heart of God and expressed the love of God by his good deed.

More Miracles in Perea

While teaching in one of the synagogues on the Sabbath day, Jesus saw a woman who was bent over and unable to lift herself up (Lk. 13:10,11). The reason Jesus gave for this woman's malady was a "spirit of infirmity" (Lk. 13:11). People often believe that sickness or a physical impairment is always biological or physiological, but in this case, this woman's bondage was the result of an evil spirit that caused her inability to stand upright. Why or how this came upon her is not revealed, but Jesus identified this bondage as illegal and unrighteous, for this woman was "a daughter of Abraham" (Lk. 13:16). She was in a covenant relationship with God as a descendent of Abraham. Therefore, she was to walk in the blessings of God and not the curse this evil enemy had brought upon her.

Jesus called to her when he saw her in the synagogue. How large the synagogue building was or how many people were in attendance is not mentioned, but this woman's condition of being bent over most likely obscured Jesus' view of her initially. Jesus, as a visiting

Rabbi (a term used to describe a teacher in Jn. 3:2 and 6:25, not necessarily one trained in the Judaic schools) would have been given the opportunity to address the congregation. At such a time, he would have been invited to sit at the front of the room while addressing the people. As Jesus was speaking, he saw this woman and immediately moved to set her free from her bondage. "Woman, you are loosed from your infirmity" (Lk. 13:12 NKJV). Jesus first set her free from the spiritual bondage that caused her infirmity and then he laid his hands on her to heal her body. Even though the evil spirit was gone, her body had been crippled because of her physical posture for all those years. Jesus laid his hands on her and healed her so she could stand upright.

The woman began to praise and glorify God for her healing but was interrupted by the ruler of the synagogue who rebuked her and instructed the people to come for healing on another day but never on the Sabbath day (Lk. 13:14). Jesus quickly challenged his elevation of the Sabbath day as being more important than this woman's deliverance with a strong rebuke, calling him, "Hypocrite". Jesus then reminded them of the chores they all perform everyday including the Sabbath, asking, "Does not each one of you on the Sabbath loose your ox or donkey from the stall, and lead it away to water it? So ought not this woman, whom Satan has bound… be loosed from this bond on the Sabbath?" (Lk. 13:15,16 NKJV). The importance of honoring the Sabbath day was not intended to limit the work of God, but to limit the work of man. Man was to rest from his own works and devote the day to worshipping God and to remembering his works of redemption. The Jewish leaders had no problem with loosing their animals to supply their own need, but stood in opposition to Jesus for loosing a woman in her need. Jesus' rebuke resulted in these leaders, identified as his adversaries, being ashamed and the people of the synagogue being free to glorify God. Truly, man was not made for the Sabbath, but the Sabbath was made for man (Mk. 2:27).

This truth regarding the Sabbath day is emphasized again when Luke shows Jesus entering the house of one of the chief Pharisees to eat bread (Lk. 14:1-6). Luke states that they "watched him". Literally, they insidiously observed him, looking for an opportunity to accuse him, and "behold, there was a certain man before him which had the dropsy" Lk. 14:2). Dropsy is an accumulation of fluid resulting in a swelling of the tissues. I don't think this man was there just by coincidence. The Pharisees had already attempted to get Jesus to leave the region by telling him that Herod was trying to kill him (Lk. 13:31). When that did not work, they devised a plan to trap Jesus by bringing a man with dropsy to the Pharisee's house. When Jesus saw the man, he immediately addressed the lawyers and Pharisees with this question, "Is it lawful to heal on the Sabbath day?" (Lk. 14:3). When they refused to answer, Jesus healed the man and sent him away. His justification for doing good to the man on the Sabbath day was compared with these religious leaders own actions regarding their animals. If you had a donkey or ox fall into a pit wouldn't you pull it out on the Sabbath day? Jesus was showing these religious schemers that they valued their livestock over a man in need.

Chapter 13

Jesus' Coming into the Land of Judea

The ministry of Jesus continued as he left Galilee and traveled through Perea on his way to Judea and ultimately the city of Jerusalem. He came into the village of Bethany (the House of Dates) just a few miles from Jerusalem on the other side of the Mount of Olives. Here he entered the house of Martha and Mary (Lk. 10:38-42). It was Martha that received him into her house, and I'm sure Jesus did not come alone but was accompanied by the twelve and possibly others. Martha's hospitality was challenged when she began preparing for all her guests, especially when her sister Mary chose to sit with the men and listen to Jesus instead of helping her in the kitchen. Martha's frustration eventually exploded into a sarcastic statement to Jesus, "Lord, don't you care that my sister has left me to serve alone?" (Lk. 10:40 CSB). Martha must have been surprised when Jesus did not immediately respond by rebuking Mary for not helping. Instead, he praised her for her desire to hear and learn what he was teaching. Mary had made the best choice, and Jesus would not take that from her. It was Martha who was full of care and "troubled about many things."

How many times do our busy schedules and obligations generate the same sarcastic prayer, though probably unspoken, "Lord, don't you care?" "Don't you care about me and what I'm going through?" Yet we fail to choose "the best part" as Mary did. Drawing aside from our troubles and cares to listen to what Jesus has to say was the best choice in Mary's day and is still true today.

The Feast of Tabernacles

It is now the middle of September, and Jesus went to Jerusalem during the Feast of Tabernacles. The Jewish leadership was watching for him and had given orders to the Temple guards to arrest him if he showed up, but in the middle of the feast, he went to Jerusalem, entered the Temple and began to teach the people (Jn. 7:14). Many had heard him before, and others had only heard about him, but now they were listening and amazed at what he was teaching (Jn. 7:15-31).

It was the last day of the feast when the multitudes came together in front of the Temple. The high priest, dressed in his royal vestments, had gone to the Pool of Siloam and filled a golden pitcher with water from the pool. As he started his procession towards the Temple, he began to quote the Psalms of ascent (Psalms 120-134). Upon reaching the steps to the Temple, the priest began declaring Isaiah 12 as he ascended the steps.

And in that day thou shalt say, O LORD, I will praise thee: though thou wast angry with me, thine anger is turned away, and thou comfortedst me. Behold, God is my salvation; I will trust, and not be afraid: for the LORD JEHOVAH is my strength and my song; he also is become my salvation. Therefore with joy shall ye draw water out of the wells of salvation. And in that day shall ye say, Praise the LORD, call upon his name, declare his doings among the people, make mention that his name is exalted. Sing unto the LORD; for he hath done excellent things: this is known in all the earth. Cry out and shout, thou inhabitant of Zion: for great is the Holy One of Israel in the midst of thee.

Then just as the high priest began to pour the water from the pitcher, Jesus shouted with a loud voice, "If any man thirst, let him come unto me, and drink. He that believeth on me as the scripture has said, out of his belly shall flow rivers of living water" (Jn. 7:37,38).

With that, many of the people said, "this is the Prophet… This is the Christ." (Jn. 7:40,41). The Pharisees, hearing the people say these things sent officers to arrest Jesus, but when they returned without him, the Pharisees asked why they did not bring him? Their only answer was, "Never man spoke like this man" (Jn. 7:46). The people were convinced that Jesus was the Christ. The Pharisees assumed the people were deceived because of their ignorance, yet it was the Pharisees who were blinded by their own jealousy and pride. Only Nicodemus defended Jesus to the Jewish council (Jn. 7:50,51).

The Pharisee's justification for rejecting Jesus as the Christ was their belief that he was from Galilee and the prophets never mentioned Galilee, but Bethlehem as the birthplace of the Christ. I wonder if anyone ever bothered to ask Jesus where he was born.

Conflict with the Scribes and Pharisees

The next day, Jesus returned to the Temple from the Mount of Olives, and it was early in the morning. He probably sat down on the steps leading up to the entrance of the Temple and began teaching the people that had gathered together. Jesus was interrupted by an angry group of scribes and Pharisees who were dragging a woman whom they made to stand in front of Jesus. "Master, this woman was taken in adultery, in the very act" said her accusers. "Now Moses in the law commanded us, that such should be stoned" (Jn. 8:4,5). It was their next words that revealed their true purpose in bringing this woman to Jesus, "but what do you say?" We know these religious leaders were attempting to get Jesus to say something against the Law of Moses so they could accuse him.

There were many things Jesus could have said to them like, "Where is the man?" Under the Law, adultery was a capital offence and both parties were to be condemned and stoned (Deut. 22:23,24), but this woman, "caught in the very act" was the only one brought before Jesus. Instead of questioning the accusers, Jesus seemingly ignored them, stooped down and wrote in the sand.

There is no record of what Jesus wrote with his finger in the sand that day, but his actions provoked the religious leaders to continue to question him. He rose up and said to them, "He that is without sin among you, let him first cast a stone at her" (Jn. 8:7). Again, he stooped down to write on the ground, ignoring the actions of the crowd. We don't know if the woman's accusers could see what Jesus was writing, but perhaps he was listing the sins of the heart such as he taught in the Sermon on the Mount: "You have heard that it is said by them of old time, You shall not commit adultery; But I say unto you, That whosoever looks on a woman to lust after her has committed adultery with her already in his heart" (Mt. 5:27).

Regardless of the exact message the words of Jesus convicted the hearts of the woman's accusers until they, one by one, left Jesus and the woman. When Jesus looked up and saw no one except the woman before him, he asked her two questions: They were "Where are [your] accusers?" and "[Has] no [one] condemned you?" (Jn. 8:10). The accusers were nowhere to be found, for their own conscience convicted them, causing them to abandon their plan. The woman answered Jesus that there was no man to condemn her. Jesus followed her answer with, "Neither do I condemn you; go, and sin no more." Once again the devious plans of the religious leaders to ensnare Jesus and embarrass him before the multitudes had failed.

Giving Sight to the Blind man

After the encounter with the Pharisees and the accused woman, Jesus continued his teaching in the Temple. The more Jesus spoke of his purpose and his submissions to the will of his Father, the more the Pharisees objected and condemned him until they took up stones to throw at him requiring him to hide from them and leave the Temple (Jn. 8:59).

Passing through the entrance leading to the Temple, he saw a man who had been blind from birth. This man's condition must have been obvious to those who saw him, for he was not just one who was blind, but was born blind. The scriptures do not explain the details, but Jesus and his disciples recognized his condition as existing since the man's birth. This man did not just have eyes that could not see, but possibly did not have any eyes, prompting the disciples to ask why this man had been born blind, suggesting that his condition had one of two causes: his parents' sin or his own (Jn. 9:1,2).

Once again Jesus had to confront the accepted idea of his day that those who were blind, sick, or had fallen into some misfortune (like the man beaten and robbed in the story of the Good Samaritan) were under the judgment of God. But Jesus said to them, "Neither [has] this man sinned, nor his parents" (Jn. 9:3). His condition was not the result of some specific sin, but when the work of God was manifested in this man, he would be blind no more.

Some have tried to use this portion of scripture to prove that God makes people sick or blind just so he can heal them and show off his power and glory. It is true that blindness has been the result of judgment against those who opposed God or the people of God in order to protect and proclaim the truth (2 Kings 6:18; Acts 13:11). However, that was a temporary blindness not designed to destroy, but to reveal the truth and goodness of God. A baby, suffering with blindness from birth and for more than forty years was not the work of God. God is righteous, and blindness is unrighteousness. Eyes were made to see, and here we see the work of God, who makes the blind to see.

The parallel Jesus uses here is that he is the "light of the world" (Jn. 9:5). He gives sight to the blind (Lk. 4:18). Healing this man's physical blindness is juxtaposed against the Pharisees' spiritual blindness (Jn. 9:40,41).

After Jesus dismisses the idea that this man's condition was his own fault or that of his parents, he spit on the ground to make clay and put it in the man's eyes. I had a student ask me one time how long I thought it took for Jesus to make clay by spitting on the ground? This man did mission work and established eye clinics so eyesight was very much a part of his ministry experience. His curiosity caused him to see for himself how long it would take to make any amount of "clay" by spitting on the ground. He told me it took more than 40 minutes to produce just a small amount of "claylike" material.

We often fail to realize the time required for some of the miracles Jesus performed. The story of the paralyzed man Jesus healed who was lowered through the roof by his four friends was not some two-minute ordeal, but they had to first "breakup" the roof to make an opening large enough to lower their friend. Likewise, this miracle of making clay also took some time. Patience had to be practiced by those witnessing the work of Jesus, and Jesus never seemed to be in a hurry. We don't know how long it may have taken Jesus to produce the clay from the spittle and put it in the man's eyes, but in this process, we have to ask ourselves, "Was Jesus applying this clay to the man's blind eyes or was he creating eyes for a man who had none?" Either way, this was a creative miracle by Jesus, but Jesus also required something of this blind man, saying, "Go, wash in the pool of Siloam" (Jn. 9:7).

I am not certain where this blind man was in relation to the pool of Siloam, but I suppose that there were other sources of water closer than walking to the pool. John makes mention in this verse the meaning of Siloam (Sent). Jesus was "sending" this blind man to the pool to wash, and his obedience was part of receiving his sight.

We often see in the stories of scripture commands that must be followed in order to see the end result. Naaman was required to dip seven times in the river Jordan to be cleansed of his leprosy (2 Kings. 5:10-14). This, seemingly foolish exercise was first rejected by Naaman. Then, his servants said to him that they were sure that, if the man of God had required him to do something difficult, he would have done it, so why not do what is easy? Naaman reconsidered and dipped in the river seven times, and the result was he no longer had leprosy. What if he had only dipped five or six times and stopped? I think he would have still been leprous because it was not the work of the water, but the result of obedience that brought Naaman his miracle.

Similarly, this blind man was sent to the pool to wash, and when he did, he received his sight. What a wonderful work of God to give this man sight. I am sure that his joy of seeing for the very first time must have left him speechless, but there were more benefits for him beyond the physical ability to see. The stigma of being under God's judgment was no longer there, and now, he could work instead of beg and enjoy the dignity of earning his own way, no more rejected by his peers, but received into the working community. This miracle of sight seemed like the greatest thing that could ever happen to this man.

When the people saw the blind man that could now see, he told them what Jesus had done for him. When they asked him where Jesus went, he did not know, so they brought him to the Pharisees, who ask him how he had received his sight. The man who had been blind explained that Jesus made clay and put it in his eyes and told him to go and wash at the pool, and when he did, he received his sight. They responded by saying that Jesus could not be of God because he made clay on the Sabbath day, thereby violating the law of God. Others argued that, if Jesus was a sinner, he could not have done such a miracle. But when the Pharisees refused to believe that the man had really been blind, they called his parents to verify that this was indeed their son and that he was born blind and to explain how he received his sight. His parents answered that he was their son and that he had been born blind, but they did not know how he received his sight (Jn. 9:8-20).

John writes that the reason they told the Pharisees what they did was because "they feared the Jews: for the Jews had agreed already, that if any man did confess that he was the Christ, he should be put out of the synagogue" (Jn. 9:22). This term "put out of the synagogue" was referencing a thirty-day suspension by the priests and the results of that suspension were dreadful. Those "put out of the synagogue" were under public scrutiny. That person would not be allowed to enter a synagogue or the Temple, to offer sacrifices. No one was allowed to speak to them, buy or sell to them. They were considered "dead" for all practical purposes during their suspension. It was a humiliating and shameful experience. The threat of this punishment was not taken lightly but provoked even this man's parents to leave him to answer for himself, fearing reprisal from the Jewish leadership.

With no cooperation from the parents, the Pharisees called the man before the council and said to him, "Give God the praise: we know that this man (referring to Jesus) is a sinner" (Jn. 9:24). The previously blind man's response has been the foundational scripture for thousands of sermons for centuries, "Whether he be a sinner or no, I know not: one thing I know, that, whereas I was blind, now I see" (Jn. 9:25). This simple but sincere retort caused the Pharisees to ask him again, "What did he do to you? How did he open your eyes?" (Jn. 9:26). Becoming aggravated by the probing of the council members, he said to them that he had already told them what happen, implying that, if they did not believe him the first time, why would they believe him if he repeated it again? The Pharisees reviled him for his comment, and after a bitter exchange, they "cast him out" (Jn. 9:34).

It is easy to read this portion of scripture and miss the severity of the Pharisees actions. The term used here, "cast him out" was not the same as "put out of the synagogue" discussed earlier. This was a total excommunication from Judaism. The man would not experience a temporary suspension but lifetime banishment. He was literally worse off now than before he was given sight. He was dead to all and without hope of salvation, being "cut off" from Israel and the promises of God. It would be difficult to imagine what was going through this man's mind. The rejection he now faced was much greater than when he was a legal, blind beggar.

Jesus had left the Temple area after healing this blind man. The scriptures do not tell us where he went, but they do tell us that Jesus heard what the Pharisees had done to the man, and immediately, he began looking for him. Jesus always had compassion for the rejected, despised, the outcast and unwanted. His message to the masses was that he had come to seek and save what was lost, to go after the lost sheep, to restore the broken hearted, and Jesus knew the overwhelming sorrow this man faced. After all, Jesus would be "despised and rejected… a man of sorrows and acquainted with grief" (Isa. 53:3).

When Jesus found the man, he said to him, "Do you believe in the Son of God?" (Jn. 9:35 MEV). There are only a few times recorded in scripture where Jesus revealed directly to someone that he was the Messiah. The man had already confessed that Jesus was of God (Jn. 9:33), but as far as we know, he had never seen Jesus with his eyes, only hearing his voice when he made the clay and sent him away. Now, he is ready to believe that Jesus is the long-awaited Messiah, asking, "Who is he Lord, that I might believe on him?" (Jn. 9:36). When Jesus revealed that he was the Messiah, the man said, "I believe. And he worshipped him." Jesus accepted this man who had been rejected and ridiculed. He may have been an outcast by society, but he was delivered out of both physical and spiritual darkness.

The Good Shepherd

The last verse of John Chapter 9 and the beginning verses of Chapter 10 are the words of Jesus as he answered the comment of the Pharisees who had heard him speak to the man they had excommunicated. Jesus had declared his purpose for coming into this world, "For judgment I am come into this world, that they which see not might see; and that they which see might be made blind" (Jn. 9:39).

"Are we blind also" was the question the Pharisees asked Jesus when they heard him say this (Jn. 9:40). To answer that question Jesus begins teaching them about his relationship to those who believe on him as the "Good Shepherd."

Jesus begins by saying to them, "If you were blind, you should have no sin; but now you say, 'We see.' Therefore, your sin remains" (Jn. 9:41). The problem with many of the Pharisees was not their spiritual blindness, not knowing who Jesus was, but their refusal to acknowledge him as their Messiah because they wanted to maintain the control they had acquired over the people. Like many people today, they were trying to find something to disqualify Jesus and defend their position. Their accusations about Jesus were false and weak, but they did not really want to know the truth therefore they were not blind, but remained in their sin.

In the following passage, Jesus creates an image of himself as the shepherd of the sheep:

> Most assuredly, I say to you, He who does not enter the sheepfold by the door, but climbs up some other way, the same is a thief and a robber. But he who enters in by the door is the shepherd of the sheep. To him the doorkeeper opens, and the sheep hear his voice; and he calls his own sheep by name and leads them out. And when he brings out his own sheep, he goes before them; and the sheep follow him, for they know his voice. Yet they will by no means follow a stranger, but will flee from him, for they do not know the voice of strangers." (Jn. 10:1-5 NKJV)

Here, Jesus is showing his listeners that he is the one who has authority to enter into the sheepfold because he is the shepherd of the sheep.

If we were to look closely at the life of a shepherd and his relationship with his sheep, we would find some amazing spiritual parallels Jesus often used to help explain his relationship with those who believed in him. For example, shepherds would often graze their sheep in the same pastures and bring the flocks together at night for the safety of the sheep. Sheep are subject to many predators (lions, wolves...) and have no defensive abilities but are dependent on the shepherds to protect them. At night, the flocks are secured in a safe enclosure as the shepherd camps at the entrance to the sheepfold. The shepherd literally becomes the entrance and porter (doorkeeper) into the sheepfold. If lions or wolves or any other predators were going to get to the sheep, they would have to first defeat the shepherd. Jesus declared, "Smite the shepherd and the sheep shall be scattered," the night he was arrested and his disciples ran from the Temple guards (Mk. 14:27).

At daybreak, the shepherds were given access to the sheepfold, and one by one, each shepherd would enter the sheepfold and call his sheep. Recognizing the familiar voice of the shepherd, the sheep would follow only their shepherd to the pasture where they would graze. Using this imagery, Jesus taught the people about who he was and why he had come.

Only the shepherd has legal access to the sheep. Anyone who attempts to get to the sheep some other way than entering by the door is a thief and a robber (Jn. 10:1,2). As the shepherd, Jesus has legally entered into the sheepfold.

There are many ideas of what Jesus meant by entering through the door into the sheepfold. Jesus was not a shepherd, and the people were not sheep, yet Jesus took considerable time here to show the people listening to him about why he had come as one with a legal right to enter the world as "the good shepherd" (vss. 11,14) and "the chief Shepherd" (1 Pet. 5:4).

In the beginning of man's existence, God reveals His purpose for creating man, "Let us make man in our image, after our likeness: and let them have dominion over…all the earth…So God created man…male and female…and God said unto them, Be fruitful, and multiply, and replenish the earth, and subdue it: and have dominion over…every living thing…" (Gen. 1:26-28). God put man in charge of the earth and gave him authority to rule God's creation. We also see from other scriptures that authority is granted to those who remain under authority. For example, the Roman centurion said, "For I am a man under authority, having soldiers under me…" (Mt. 8:9). The centurion was to command the soldiers under him as a representative of Rome. As long as the Roman government authorized the centurion's commands, he was enforcing the will of Rome by his authority. If the centurion disobeyed the commands of his Roman superiors and gave orders for his men to do what was contrary to the will of Rome, he would be subverting his authority for his own purposes or those of another. Likewise, God gave man authority to command his creation as long as man was submitted to the authority of God, but God warned man, "But of the tree of the knowledge of good and evil, you shall not eat: for in the day that you eat of it you shall surely die" (Gen. 2:17 NKJV).

We read that scripture and can initially assume that, the moment Adam sinned (rebelled against the authority of God by disobedience), he would immediately die and be buried because his days were over. But we discover that Adam lived nine hundred and thirty years (Gen. 5:5), many years after he sinned by eating of the forbidden fruit. So Adam's dying after eating of the tree was not physical but spiritual death, and his God given authority was hijacked by the devil for his own purposes.

In the temptation in the wilderness, Jesus was taken by Satan to a lofty place and shown all the kingdoms of the world. Satan said to Jesus that he would give him all the authority and the glory of them, for that had been delivered unto him to give it to whomsoever he will (Lk. 4:5,6). Now my question is, "Who gave Satan the authority over the kingdoms of the world?" It surely was not God because God had given man authority over his creation. In fact, the psalmist declares, "The heaven, even the heavens, are the Lord's; but the earth has he given to the children of men" (Ps. 115:16). Therefore, we see that authority was given to man to do God's will, but we also find in the Book of Romans this truth. Paul writes, "Don't you know, that to whom you yield yourselves servants to obey, his servants you are to whom you obey; whether of sin unto death, or of obedience unto righteousness?" (Rom. 6:16).

The day Adam sinned, he became the servant of Satan by obeying him and disobeying God. The authority God had given man was now yielded to a wicked and rebellious spirit. Satan could not just go and do whatever he pleased, but if he could get man to do what he pleased with the authority God had given him, Satan could then pervert what God had given man for his own purposes. Jesus emphasized this truth when he said to the Jews who sought to kill him, "[You] are of your father the devil, and the lusts of your father [you] will do. He was a murderer from the beginning, and abode not in the truth, because there is no truth in him. When he [speaks] a lie, he [speaks] of his own: for he is a liar, and the father of it" (Jn. 8:44). We see that the Jewish leaders were being influenced by Satan to use the authority they had to do his will and destroy Jesus. But Jesus also had authority unpolluted and undefiled. Sinful man's authority had been corrupted, but Jesus was not born of Adam's sinful nature. The people marveled at Jesus when they heard him speak and when he healed the sick or cast out unclean spirits, saying, "What thing is this? What new doctrine is this? For with authority he commands even the unclean spirits, and they obey him" (Mk. 1:28). Luke records that the people were "all amazed, and spoke among themselves, saying, 'What a word is this! For with authority and power he commands the unclean spirits, and they come out'" (Lk. 4:36).

The authority Jesus walked in was given to him, not because he was the Son of God, but because he was the Son of man. The gospel of John tells us, "For as the Father has life in himself; so has he given to the Son to have life in himself; And has given him authority to execute judgment also, because he is the Son of man" (Jn. 5:26,27). Jesus was walking in the righteous authority God had given man in the beginning. No wonder Jesus is called the "Second man" (1 Cor. 15:47). The first man was Adam, and he disobeyed God and yielded to Satan and sin. Jesus, the second man, walking blameless and sinless before God always obeyed his Father (Jn. 6:38; 8:29). Jesus had the right (authority) to enter the sheepfold as the Shepherd of the sheep. He would lead his sheep into "green pastures" and "beside still waters" (Ps. 23:2). His sheep would hear his voice and follow him. In contrast, the Jewish leaders only heard his voice as a "stranger" and not as the shepherd (Jn. 10:4,5).

As Jesus continued with this parable, he said, "I am the door of the sheep" (Jn. 10:7). Later, Jesus said, "I am the way, the truth, and the life: no man comes to the Father, but by me" (Jn. 14:6). The contrast of Jesus as the good shepherd with the thief shows the purpose of a thief is to "steal, …kill, and… destroy" (Jn. 10:10), but the purpose of the good shepherd is to give abundant life.

Satan used man's authority against him, and as a liar, a thief, and a murderer, he attempted to destroy man and God's purpose for him. Jesus came into the world as the Good Shepherd who gives his life for the sheep, a very different motivation. The Jewish leaders are described here as the hirelings. Their only purpose is to get a paycheck at the end of their shift. They are not willing to fight off the wolves and lions to protect the sheep. Running to save themselves, they leave the sheep to be scattered and destroyed.

Right in the middle of this teaching, Jesus gave some insight into the purpose of God for all the Gentile nations and not just the Jews. He said, "Other sheep I have, which are not of this fold: them also I must bring, and they shall hear my voice, and there shall be one fold, and one shepherd" (Jn. 10:16). When Jesus sent out the apostles he told them to go only to the lost sheep of Israel (Mt. 10:6). When the Canaanite woman came to Jesus looking for help to heal her daughter, Jesus told her, "I am not sent but unto the lost sheep of the house of Israel" (Mt. 15:24).

Jesus was the Jewish Messiah, but in him would all the nations be blessed (Ps. 72:17; Gal. 3:8). Once Jesus fulfilled the promises to the house of Israel, he had completed the work of redemption for all humanity. After the resurrection, Jesus gave the great commission to "Go… and make disciples of all nations…" (Mt. 28:19). Apparently, since the first converts were Jewish believers, the church took on the belief that Jesus meant to go to all of the Jewish nations. It wasn't until Peter took the gospel to the Gentile Cornelius and all his family and friends who were saved and filled with the Spirit that he said, "Of a truth I perceive that God is no respecter of persons: But in every nation he that fears him, and work[s] righteousness, is accepted with him" (Acts 10:34,35). Later, Peter had to defend his actions of going to a Gentile's house to the church at Jerusalem. When they heard what God had done, they said, "Then has God also to the Gentiles granted repentance unto life" (Acts 11:18). Jesus had "other sheep" that were not of the Jewish fold, but he would bring them and they shall hear his voice and there shall be one fold and one shepherd (Jn. 10:16).

After this teaching, which was during the Feast of Dedication (Hanukkah), the Jews directly asked Jesus, "If you are the Christ, tell us plainly" (Jn. 10:24 NET). His answer that he was one with God incited such a riot in Jerusalem that Jesus had to escape out of their hand for they sought to arrest him (Jn. 10:39). Leaving Jerusalem, Jesus traveled with his disciples to Bethabara beyond the Jordan River.

Raising Lazarus

While Jesus was at Bethabara, he received word that his friend Lazarus was very sick. Lazarus was the brother of Martha and Mary mentioned in Luke chapter ten. The dinner Martha hosted for Jesus and his disciples may have been the initial meeting with this family, but the friendship Jesus had with Martha, Mary, and Lazarus must have continued because they were greatly loved by Jesus (Jn. 11:5).

John often times writes a short commentary about certain events in his gospel, and he tells us in this portion of scripture that it was Martha's and Lazarus' sister Mary that would shortly anoint Jesus with the expensive oil (Jn. 12:3). This event had not happened yet, John simply notifies his readers which Mary this was.

Lazarus and his sisters lived in Bethany near Jerusalem where Jesus and his disciples had just recently escaped from the Jewish leaders who, with rocks in their hands, threatened Jesus with death, accusing him of blasphemy (Jn. 10:32-39). Now Jesus was some twenty miles from Jerusalem, but must have told Mary and Martha where he was going because they knew where to find him when Lazarus became ill.

When Jesus received the message concerning Lazarus, he said to his disciples, "This sickness is not unto death…" (Jn. 11:4). Jesus knew Lazarus would die and that he would raise him from the dead and the result of this miracle would bring glory to God.

Some have mistakenly understood that God made Lazarus sick just so he could die and be raised from the dead to show the world that Jesus was the Messiah. But sickness is part of the curse Jesus bore for us, not a tool of God. The end result of this miracle would bring much glory to God, but God knows how to accomplish his will and protect those who will trust him. If Jesus returned to Bethany just down the road from Jerusalem, the Jews would be waiting for him, and I'm sure they would still have rocks in their hands. Although Jesus had avoided the Jews and fled the city, news of his friend Lazarus's illness would have caused them to expect Jesus to return to heal his friend.

After hearing the news about Lazarus, Jesus remained near the Jordan River for several days until Jesus said to his disciples, "Let us go into Judea again" (Jn. 11:7). Their response to his statement was filled with fear of what might happen if they returned. "Rabbi, lately the Jews sought to stone You; and are You going there again?" (Jn. 11:8 NKJV). Jesus took this opportunity to teach them about hearing from God and walking in the revelation he brings. It may have seemed to be a dangerous decision to return to Judea, but Jesus said to them, "Lazarus is dead…nevertheless let us go unto him" (Jn. 11:14,15). It was Thomas that said to the other disciples, "Let us also go that we may die with him" (Jn. 11:16). They were expecting trouble if they returned, but what they did not know was that Lazarus had already been dead for several days. If the Jews who were seeking to kill Jesus had been waiting for him to return and heal his friend, they would have, by this time, determined that he was not going to come because Lazarus was dead and in the tomb.

Following the leading of the Holy Spirit and the voice of his Father, Jesus could return with confidence. The timing was right, and he was walking in the light (of God's leading). Therefore, he would not be stumbling in the dark (not knowing when to return).

Upon his return to Bethany, a messenger brought news to Martha, who was sitting in the house that Jesus was on his way. She immediately got up and ran to meet him. Martha greeted Jesus with a tone of accusation, "Lord, if you had been here, my brother would not have died" (Jn. 11:21 NKJV). But she continued with a great statement of faith, "But even now I know that whatever You ask of God, God will give You" (Jn. 11:22 MEV). Jesus replied by saying, "[Your] brother will rise again" (Jn. 11:23), a declaration that should have invoked great hope in Martha, but instead she responds with, "I know that he shall rise again in the resurrection at the last day" (Jn. 11:24). It seems that Martha's temporary faith gave way to the realization that her brother had already been dead and buried for four days. Recalling some previous teaching of Jesus about a future resurrection, Martha seems to have lost any hope of seeing her brother until that future day.

Jesus continued to remind her that he is the resurrection and life and that those who believe in him will never die. Martha acknowledged that she believed that he was the Christ, but she returned to the house and told Mary that Jesus had arrived, and he was asking about her. Upon hearing that Jesus had returned, Mary quickly left the house and ran to where Jesus was. Many friends who were also in the house followed Mary, thinking that she was going to the tomb to weep. After hurrying to the place where Jesus was, she fell at his feet in respect but brought the same tone of accusation, saying, "Lord, if You had been here, my brother would not have died" (Jn. 11:32 NKJV). Jesus was clearly touched with the sadness of the sisters and their friends. Sighing deeply, he asked to see the tomb where they had placed the body (Jn. 11:33).

People have questioned why Jesus would weep when he knew he was about to raise Lazarus from the dead. Although he knew the happy outcome, his compassion for Martha and Mary demonstrated his empathy for those facing trouble, hardship, or sorrow. "For we do not have a High Priest who cannot sympathize with our weaknesses..." (Heb. 4:15 NKJV).

How amazing it is to know that God does not ignore our hurts, pains, and sorrows, but he is moved to tears with the sorrows we face.

When Jesus called for the stone that covered the mouth of the tomb to be removed, Martha immediately complained, "Lord, by this time he [stinks]: for he [has] been dead four days" (Jn. 11:39). Sensing Martha's fear of seeing her brother's body in a state of decomposition, Jesus said to her, "Didn't I tell you that if you believed you would see the glory of God?" (Jn. 11:40 CSB). Martha then must have approved of the removing of the stone, for they took it away from the entrance. After a short prayer, Jesus cried with a loud voice, "Lazarus, come out" (Jn. 11:43 AMP). We are not given the details of how Lazarus stood up, being bound hand and foot with grave clothes, but he rose up and made his way to the mouth of the tomb even though his eyes were covered with a cloth.

I've often wondered what Lazarus must have thought when he opened his eyes and realized he was bound and unable to see what was going on. His last recollection must have been of the room in the house where he died. Now, he had no idea where he was or why he was there. But the familiar sound of the voice of Jesus was calling to him to "come out". If he had been buried according to the custom of the Jews, his body would have been wrapped in strips of cloth that had been soaked in a solution that, after four days, would have hardened like plaster of Paris (Lk. 23:55-24:1), or he may have just been wrapped in the grave clothes without the spices and ointments as Ananias (Acts 5:6). Either way he was tightly wrapped in the grave clothes from head to foot. How he managed to rise up and make his way to the entrance of the tomb is not known, but the miracle was so widely talked about that the Jewish leaders discussed the possibility of putting Lazarus to death because so many people came to see him after he arose from the dead and believed on Jesus (Jn. 12:9-11).

What a happy reunion it must have been for Martha and Mary to have their brother with them again. Many of the Jews who were friends with Mary saw this miracle, and they believed on Jesus; however, others who saw it went to the Pharisees and told them what Jesus had done (Jn. 11:45,46). Instead of being awed by the miracle, the Pharisees called the council together to devise a plan to arrest Jesus and put him to death; Jesus, therefore, left the city and went to the wilderness city of Ephraim near Jericho (Jn. 11:54).

Blind Bartimaeus

As Jesus and his disciples passed through Jericho in the company of many people, he heard someone call to him, saying, "Jesus, thou son of David, have mercy on me" (Mk. 10:47). Most likely, many people were calling out to Jesus, but this voice was recognizing Jesus as the son of David, a Messianic term. Jesus stopped abruptly and called the man to come to him, not knowing his condition. The crowd had previously scolded the man, trying to keep him quiet, but now, after Jesus invited him to come to him, the onlookers said to the man, "Be of good comfort. Rise, he is calling you" (Mk. 10:49 MEV). Mark records in his gospel that the man "casting away his garment, rose, and came to Jesus" (10:50).

The significance of this man throwing away his garment might easily be overlooked because this wasn't just any garment. As a beggar, the Jewish council, identifying his condition as legitimate, would have issued this man a particular garment. It would have been much like our handicap parking sticker, allowing those who have been authenticated as truly handicapped to park where others would be fined. This was a valuable garment for a beggar who could, potentially receive many more alms than others whose limitations may be questioned. By throwing away this garment, the man was stepping out in faith, believing he was about to receive his sight. His action of faith was noted by Jesus, who, after hearing what he wanted, declared, "[your] faith has made [you] whole" (Mk. 10:52). Immediately the man received his sight and followed Jesus leaving his beggar's cloak behind.

Zacchaeus

The word that Jesus and his disciples were passing through the city of Jericho brought the crowds of people together in the streets. Soon the warm spring air of the desert countryside was filled with voices of the people who must have heard of the blind beggar Jesus healed on his way into the city. Because of the crowded streets, it was difficult for anyone to get a good look at Jesus except for those closest to him. That was especially true of the chief tax collector of the city, a man named Zacchaeus, who was very short in stature (Lk.19:1-4). Zacchaeus must have heard about the many miracles Jesus had performed, and perhaps, he also heard that the religious leaders called Jesus a "friend of publicans [tax collectors] and sinners" (Lk. 7:34). This title given to Jesus by the religious leaders was not complimentary for the tax collectors were considered to be traitors to Israel, for they worked for the Roman government, collecting taxes of the people and were known for collecting more than the people were required to pay, filling their own pockets with the proceeds. This made the tax collectors despised by the people and yet very wealthy. Maybe Zacchaeus had heard that Matthew, one of Jesus' own disciples was a former tax collector. For whatever the reason, Zacchaeus ran ahead of Jesus and the crowd of people and climbed up into a tree, waiting for Jesus to pass near him. When Jesus came to the place, he looked up and saw Zacchaeus and called him by name, "Zacchaeus, make haste, and come down; for to day I must abide at your house" (Lk. 19:5). Zacchaeus hurried down from the tree and received Jesus with great joy.

The fickleness of the people was revealed when their shouts of praise quickly become murmurings against Jesus because he would share lunch with a man they all considered unworthy and unclean. But Jesus' mission was to bring salvation to the sons of Abraham, "to seek and save that which was lost" (Lk. 19:10). Jesus was often drawn to the despised and rejected to restore them to a pure relationship with God. Perhaps this was what Jesus saw in Zacchaeus, whose name means "innocent" or "pure," for Zacchaeus said to Jesus that afternoon, "Behold, Lord, the half of my goods I give to the poor; and if I have taken any thing from any man by false accusation, I restore him fourfold (Lk. 19:8). Truly salvation had come to Zacchaeus' house that day.

Jesus Entering Jerusalem

Leaving Jericho, Jesus and the disciples make the twenty-mile trip across the desert to Bethphage, near the Mount of Olives. On the east side of the city of Jerusalem was the Kidron valley, which separated the Temple mount from the Mount of Olives. Just east of the mount were the towns of Bethphage and Bethany.

From the Mount of Olives, Jesus could clearly see the city of Jerusalem and the Temple. He sent two of his disciples to the nearby town of Bethphage to acquire a donkey and its colt. There is no record of Jesus making arrangements for the animals, but having many friends in Bethany and Bethphage, he may have ask Lazarus or Simon the leper to have the animals ready. Regardless of the process the disciples found the donkey and her colt tied up at the first intersection as they entered the village. After bringing them to Jesus, they covered the colt and the donkey with their cloaks before Jesus sat on the colt (Mt. 21:1-7; Mk. 11:1-7).

Donkeys were used as beasts of burden to carry heavy loads or to ride upon, but it is said of this colt that no one had ever ridden it (Mk. 11:2). Knowing a few things about horses and donkeys, I can say that one does not just cinch up a saddle and jump on without significant preparation. I can't see Jesus riding a donkey bucking and kicking down the mountainside. So this man who calmed the sea with a word and delivered the sick and oppressed because of the anointing he carried was able to elicit peace and cooperation from a young animal that would fulfill the words of the prophet Zechariah spoken so many centuries before.

> "Rejoice greatly, O daughter of Zion!
> Shout, O daughter of Jerusalem!
> Behold, your King is coming to you;
> He is just, and having salvation,
> Lowly, and riding on a donkey,
> A colt, the foal of a donkey." (Zech. 9:9 NKJV)

Jesus began his descent from the mount of Olives mounted on the donkey as many people began to gather and spread their clothes in the path while others cut palm branches to create a carpet for the royal ambassador bringing his message of hope to a city he knew would reject his words. As Jesus rode toward the city, his many disciples began to rejoice, shouting, "Blessed be the King that comes in the name of the Lord: peace in heaven, and glory in the highest. Hosanna; Blessed is he that comes in the name of the Lord: Blessed be the kingdom of our father David, that comes in the name of the Lord; Hosanna in the highest" (Mk. 11:9,10). Luke records the people shouting similar praises (19:38).

Some of the Pharisees who were among the multitudes came to Jesus attempting to get him to command the people to cease their praises of him. Jesus warned them that, if the people ceased praising him, that the stones themselves would cry out. Jesus then beheld the city that would very soon crucify and kill him, and he wept over it. His weeping was not for the anticipated suffering he would endure but for the destruction of the city their rejection of him would bring upon them (Lk. 19:41-44). The religious leaders' rejection would eventually cause the Temple and all the city of Jerusalem to be destroyed, leaving not even "one stone upon another" (Mt. 24:2). As the praises of the multitudes brought peace to the city, so the rejection of their Messiah would cause the stones that composed the city to be thrown down. Forty years later, these stones lay in rubble, yet they still brought praise that recognized Jesus as Lord and confirmed his prophetic word as true.

Cursing the Fig Tree

After being carried into the city of Jerusalem on the young beast of burden, Jesus dismounted and went into the Temple. It was now late in the day, so after a brief observation of what was going on in the Temple, Jesus left the city to spend the night in Bethany. In the morning Jesus left Bethany on his way to the Temple. While passing through Bethphage (House of figs), he saw a fig tree in the distance. Hungry and anticipating the taste of the fruit, he approached the tree, only to find leaves but no fruit. Since fruit forms before the leaves on a fig tree and the harvesting of the fruit had not yet been done, Jesus would have expected this tree to have plenty of fruit, but there was none. As a result, Jesus cursed the barren tree, saying, "No one will ever eat fruit from you again." (Mk. 11:14 AMP).

Jesus continued with his disciples to the Temple, but instead of teaching the crowds there, he entered the outer court where the currency brokers had tables filled with coins. Sacrificial animals were being bought and sold, and this court of prayer had become a place of merchandise. Quickly, Jesus began to chase the merchants and the animals out of the Temple, turning over the tables as coins roll in every direction. Not allowing anyone to carry any of these things out of the Temple court, Jesus was, once again, fulfilling the words of the prophets saying, "Is it not written, My house shall be called of all nations the house of prayer? But [you] have made it a den of thieves" (Mk. 11:17).

This was the second time Jesus had cleansed the Temple. John's gospel shows Jesus cleansing the Temple in this very same way at the beginning of his ministry (Jn. 2:14-16). How appropriate that the first Passover as the Christ (Anointed One) and the last Jesus would purge his Father's house from the merchants that were literally robbing the people, requiring their Roman currencies to be changed to Temple currency before purchasing the only animals approved for sacrifice. The inflated costs robbed the people of their money, but even more tragic than that was robbing the people of prayer. After the outer court was once again prepared as a place of prayer those in need came to Jesus where the lame and blind were healed (Mt. 21:14). Jesus must have spent most of the day ministering to the needs of the people because after a brief encounter with the scribes and chief priests it was late afternoon and Jesus went out of the city returning to Bethany for the night with his disciples (Mk. 11:18,19).

The next morning Jesus and his disciples returned to the Temple from Bethany, passing by the fig tree Jesus had cursed. Peter seeing the fig tree "dried up from the roots," draws Jesus' attention to the tree, reminding him what he had done the day before. Jesus responded to Peter and all the disciples saying,

> Have faith in God. For assuredly, I say to you, whoever says to this mountain, "Be removed and be cast into the sea," and does not doubt in his heart, but believes that those things he says will be done, he will have whatever he says. Therefore I say

to you, whatever things you ask when you pray, believe that you receive them, and you will have them (Mk. 11:22-24).

Many translators have understood the "have faith in God" to, more literally say, "have the faith of God". While it is obvious that we must have faith in God for "without faith it is impossible to please God" (Heb. 11:6), the faith we have is God's faith. If God's kind of faith comes to us by "hearing... the word of God" (Rom. 10:17), then the faith we receive is truly God's faith. God's faith is a gift to us (Eph. 2:8), and because it is God's faith it is powerful. Speaking to mountains, either literal or figurative, those with the faith of God see not only what they say accomplished, but they also receive whatever they require.

Jesus was using the withered fig tree as an example of what he expected his disciples to do by the power of the prayer of faith. But his instruction to them did not end with verse 24, for the following two verses are also a requirement for this display of God's power. "And whenever you stand praying, if you have anything against anyone, forgive him, that your Father in heaven may also forgive you your trespasses. But if you do not forgive, neither will your Father in heaven forgive your trespasses" (Mk. 11:25,26 NKJV).

The unfounded and deceitful attacks against Jesus would be something that his disciples would soon experience. Jesus was about to go to the cross and pay the price required for the forgiveness of sins for all humanity. If God forgives sins because of the blood of Jesus then neither should we hold on to the sins and offences of others. As long as we choose not to forgive others, regardless of their unrighteous acts against us, we are saying that what Jesus did to pay for that sin was not enough for us. Refusing to forgive anyone brings condemnation, and if our hearts condemn us, then we will have no confidence or faith towards God (1 Jn. 3:21). The faith of God does not work in a heart full of condemnation. If the devil wanted to shut off the power of God in the lives of the disciples of Jesus, then provoking them through unrighteous persecution from others would do the job. Being hateful, bitter, without forgiveness for someone who has purposefully and unmercifully hurt and wounded us is a natural and worldly response. If we use our wounds as an excuse to hold others in contempt, then we ignore the wounds of Jesus and allow our enemy to keep us powerless to overcome his works or to give evidence to the power and love of God. Jesus was instructing his disciples on how to protect their hearts and pray the prayer of faith that could move mountains and accomplish the will of God.

CHAPTER 14

PARABLES OF JUDGMENT AND THE DESTRUCTION OF JERUSALEM

Jesus was daily at the Temple, speaking to the people by parables. The parable of the vineyard was presented by Jesus to the chief priests and elders. He described a man who owned a vineyard and leased it to vinedressers to care for the vineyard until the time of harvest. When the fruit was ready for harvest, the owner of the vineyard sent his servants to receive the fruit, but the vinedressers rejected the servants, beating some, stoning and killing others. After sending numerous servants, the owner decides to send his son to receive the fruit, believing the vinedressers would honor his son. When the vinedressers saw the son coming, they plotted to kill him, thinking they would acquire the vineyard for themselves. After seizing and dragging the son out of the vineyard, they kill him. Then, Jesus asked these religious leaders, "[W]hen the owner of the vineyard comes, what will he do to those vinedressers?" (Mt. 21:40 NKJV). Immediately, the religious leaders say to Jesus, "He will destroy those wicked men miserably, and lease his vineyard to other vinedressers who will render to him the fruits in their seasons" (Mt. 21:41 NKJV). Jesus then said to them:

> "Have you never read in the Scriptures
> 'The stone which the builders rejected
> Has become the chief cornerstone.
> This was the Lord's doing,
> And it is marvelous in our eyes? (Mt. 21:42; Ps. 118:22,23 NKJV).
>
> Therefore I say to you, the kingdom of God will be taken from you and given to a nation bearing the fruits of it. And whoever falls on this stone will be broken; but on whomever it falls, it will grind him to powder" (Mt. 21:43,44 NKJV).

Jesus was making the meaning of this parable very plain. The vineyard is the kingdom of God, and the owner is God. The vinedressers are the religious leaders of Israel, and the servants who were sent were the prophets. They were beaten, imprisoned, and killed by the religious leaders until God sent his son, Jesus. The fate of those who reject Jesus is their destruction by the very one that becomes the chief cornerstone (Jesus, the foundation of the true Temple of God – the church), whose revealed word becomes the immovable foundation of the kingdom God (Mt. 7:24-27; 16:16-19).

Once the chief priest and Pharisees understood that Jesus was speaking about them in this parable, they sought to arrest him, but they could not because they feared the people who believed Jesus to be a prophet. However, Jesus continued in the Temple, speaking to the people by parables as the hostility of the Jewish leaders escalated more and more until Jesus began a declaration of woes against these vile leaders.

"Woe unto you, scribes and Pharisees, hypocrites!" (Mt. 23:13,14,15)

"Woe unto you… blind guides" (Mt. 23:16)

"Woe unto you, scribes and Pharisees, hypocrites! (Mt. 23:23,25,27,29,)

"[You] serpents, you generation of vipers" (Mt. 23:33)

And then Jesus declared a powerful prophetic word, announcing what was about to happen,

"I send you prophets, wise men, and scribes: some of them you will kill and crucify, and some of them you will scourge in your synagogues and persecute from city to city, that on you may come all the righteous blood shed on the earth, from the blood of righteous Abel to the blood of Zechariah, son of Berechiah, whom you murdered between the temple and the altar, Assuredly I say to you, all these things will come upon this generation" (Mt. 23:34-36 NKJV).

Judgment was not God's will for his people, for Jesus spoke of what could have been, "How often I wanted to gather your children together, as a hen gathers her chicks under her wings, but you were not willing!" (Mt. 23:37 NKJV). Therefore, the destruction of the city of Jerusalem would soon be a reality, Jesus said, "[Your] house is left to you desolate" (Mt. 23:38).

Here Jesus also told the Jewish leaders that they would not see him again until they recognized that he truly came in the name of the Lord. But that day would be a day of judgment, fulfilling his words of warning. Jesus was not saying that these scribes and Pharisees would never see him again from that day, for they would continue to pursue him until the Feast of Passover which was later that same week when he was arrested, tried and crucified. But Jesus was saying that, after he was slain, they would not see him again until he would return in judgment, fulfilling the prophetic word he had just spoken to them. Then they would know who he really was and that he truly came in the name of the Lord.

What a remarkable warning, and declaration of judgment that would end in the total desolation of Jerusalem and the Temple. Jesus then left the Temple just as his disciples came desiring him to come with them to look at the new construction taking place on the Temple buildings.

Some have inquired why the disciples wanted Jesus to see the Temple he had visited yearly since his birth. Wouldn't he have seen all the buildings of the Temple multiple times? This grand Temple began as a project by king Herod some forty-six years earlier and would not be fully completed until A.D. 64, another 34 years from this time. It was the new construction the disciples of Jesus wanted him to see. It was at this time Jesus said to them, "Do you not see all these things? Assuredly, I say to you, not one stone shall be left here upon another, that shall not be thrown down" (Mt. 24:2 NKJV).

Jesus and his disciples made their way to the Mount of Olives where they sat down facing the city and the Temple mount. The disciples asked Jesus to explain to them the time frame of his prophetic word, saying, "Tell us, when shall these things be? And what shall be the sign of [your] coming, and of the end of the world?" (Mt. 24:3).

Jesus had already said that this judgment would come upon that generation when the Temple and city would be destroyed. This judgment would be terrible for it was what was required for all the righteous blood shed on the earth beginning with Abel. The righteous blood was in reference to all the prophets God had sent to his people. Abel, the son of Adam and the brother of Cain, was the first prophet to be slain. The last would be those servants of God up until this word was fulfilled in A.D. 70. This great judgment included the blood of Jesus, for the people foolishly declared to Pilate at the trial of Jesus, "His blood be on us, and on our children" (Mt. 27:25).

The events of Matthew 24 really have nothing to do with the "end of the world." That phrase more literally says, "the end of the age." The word-translated *world* here is *aion*, which means age. God gave Israel forty years to repent before great judgment would fall, ending the age of the Temple worship. The new covenant had no need of a temple made by man because God, by his Spirit, had moved into the bodies of believers, and therefore, their assembly, the church, became his temple.

Jesus said that the generation to whom he was speaking would experience all these things. A generation is measured typically in scripture as forty years. The "generation" that came out of Egypt died in the wilderness. They wandered in the desert for forty years. Also, in the first chapter of Matthew, fourteen generations are mentioned between significant events. He writes, "So all the generations from Abraham to David are fourteen generations; and from David until the carrying away into Babylon are fourteen generations; and from the carrying away into Babylon unto Christ are fourteen generations" (1:17). If we measure a generation as forty years, then the fourteen generations mentioned in Matthew's gospel fit the timeframe perfectly. Jesus was crucified and resurrected in the year A.D. 30 and exactly forty years later, A.D. 70 the Roman general Titus destroyed the city of Jerusalem and the Temple.

Much of the language in Matthew twenty-four sounds very apocalyptic with the sun being darkened and the stars falling from heaven and the Son of man coming in the clouds of heaven, but this language describing terrible judgment is referring to the city's and the temple's destruction. This same language is used often to describe God's impending judgment on kingdoms and cities throughout the centuries. God's judgment on Babylon is described in Isaiah, "For the stars of heaven and the constellations thereof shall not give their light: the sun shall be darkened in his going forth, and the moon shall not cause her light to shine" (Isa. 13:10). Later, Isaiah again describes the soon coming judgment on Egypt, saying,

> "…Behold, the Lord rides upon a swift cloud,
> and shall come into Egypt:
> and the idols of Egypt shall be moved at his presence,
> and the heart of Egypt shall melt in the midst of it." (Isa. 19:1).

Similarly, Jesus told the high priest of his day that he would see him coming in clouds of heaven, announcing, "…Hereafter shall you see the Son of man sitting on the right hand of power and coming in the clouds of heaven" (Mt. 26:64). Jesus also describes to his disciples the terrible coming judgment and tribulation when the city and Temple are destroyed and answers their question about when these things shall be, saying, "…This generation shall not pass, till all these things be fulfilled." (Mt. 24:34).

Chapter 15

Jesus Anointed for Burial

As Passover approaches the chief priests and the Pharisees had given a command that if anyone knew where Jesus was they should show them (Jn. 11:57). Their intentions were to have him arrested on the false grounds of blasphemy because he had embarrassed and exposed them at the temple. It is important for us to understand the disposition of the religious leaders and the event that occurred prior to this with Judas who was with Jesus in Bethany.

Jesus had been staying in Bethany during the time he was teaching the people at the temple. The gospels show us that the house of Martha, Mary, and Lazarus was there as well as the house of Simon the leper. We know nothing about Simon except that he must have been healed by Jesus of leprosy and was acquainted with Martha and her family because, six days prior to the Passover feast, Jesus was having dinner with Simon and Lazarus, and Martha and Mary were there (Jn. 12:1-8). During the course of the dinner, Mary came to Jesus as he was reclining at the table and began to anoint his feet with a very costly ointment (perfumed oil).

Both Matthew and Mark's gospels describe this same event without naming Mary and both record that this woman anointed Jesus' head. The timeframe, place, events, and results are the same in all three gospels, so there is no reason to believe that Jesus was anointed twice in this fashion. Only Matthew and Mark's accounts record the anointing of Jesus' head while John's gospel records the anointing of his feet. Jesus simply says of Mary, "For in that she hath poured this ointment on my body, she did it for my burial" (Mt. 26:12). Mark 14:8 records the words of Jesus as "she is come aforehand to anoint my body to the burying."

It was customary to anoint the dead before burial, but to pour such expensive oil upon Jesus was considered wasteful as he was very much alive and eating dinner with his friends. It was Judas Iscariot who led the complaint against Mary saying, "Why was not this ointment sold for three hundred pence, and given to the poor?" (Jn. 12:5). The next verse explains why Judas said this and what was really in his heart, "This he said, not that he cared for the poor; but because he was a thief, and had the bag, and bare what was put therein" (Jn. 12:6).

Although Jesus knew from the very beginning that Judas would betray him (Jn. 6:64), he still gave Judas a place of responsibility among his ministry team. Judas was the treasurer for Jesus' ministry but here it is revealed that he was a thief and stole from the ministry funds.

His accusation against Mary caused Jesus to come to her defense. "Let her alone; why do you trouble her?" (Mk. 14:6-9). Obviously, Judas' open rebuke of Mary caused her to be troubled. Jesus continued to commend her for her sacrifice and declared that her deed was good and necessary showing that he would soon be buried, but what she had done would be memorialized throughout the whole world everywhere the gospel was preached (Mk. 14:7-9).

Mary probably had no idea that her pouring this oil upon Jesus' head and feet was a prompting of the Holy Spirit. For this act foretold of Jesus' death and burial and was the event that would reveal who Judas really was and what would prompt him to go to the religious leaders and betray Jesus (Mk. 14:10,11).

Judas may have believed that Jesus, as the Messiah, would do what many of the Jews believed the Messiah would do when he appeared. He would overthrow the Romans and establish again the kingdom of Israel (Acts 1:6), and Judas would be one of the twelve sitting on a throne, judging the twelve tribes of Israel (Lk. 22:28-30). When Judas understood that Jesus is going to die and be buried and his kingdom was spiritual not political, his expectations were shattered. Looking for a reward for his actions, Judas went to the chief priests and agreed to hand Jesus over to them for thirty pieces of silver (Mt. 26:14-16).

I wonder if things could have been different if Judas had known the prophesy of Zechariah five-hundred years earlier (Zech. 11:12,13). The Messiah would be betrayed for thirty pieces of silver but those silver coins would end up being cast into the Temple to buy the potter's field to bury the poor. Judas himself may have been buried in the very field those coins purchased (Mt. 27:3-10; Acts 1:16-20).

Chapter 16

Preparation for Passover

When the time for the Passover feast had come, the disciples of Jesus asked him, "Where do You want us to go and prepare for You to eat the Passover?" (Mk. 14:12 AMP).

The Jews measured days from sundown to sundown as is described in the Book of Genesis, "And the evening and the morning were the first day" (Gen. 1:5). So the day of the preparation for the Feast of Passover began at sundown. The lamb would be slain at 3:00 PM the following afternoon. It was prior to the going down of the sun that the disciples enquired of Jesus where they were to eat the Passover meal. Jesus knew that Judas was looking for an opportunity to betray him to the Jews, so instead of announcing the location where he would be alone with the twelve, he called two of them, not Judas, to go into the city of Jerusalem, and there they would meet a man carrying a pitcher of water, and he would show them the place where they could prepare the meal. Jesus must have made these preparations ahead of time to keep this address a secret, for he did not want to be interrupted before he ate the Passover meal with the twelve.

When the evening had come and Jesus and his disciples were in a large, furnished upper room, preparing to eat the Passover meal, Jesus said to them, "With desire I have desired to eat this Passover with you before I suffer: for I say unto you, I will not any more eat thereof, until it be fulfilled in the kingdom of God" (Lk. 22:15,16). Jesus is saying that he is about to suffer. He is the Lamb of God and surely he will be slain at 3:00 PM the next afternoon.

Jesus would first eat the Passover meal with the twelve (Lk. 22:17,18). What happened next is described only in John's gospel. After supper, Jesus lay aside his outer garments and took a towel, poured water into a basin, and began washing his disciples' feet and drying them with the towel (Jn. 13:2-5). This action by Jesus may have been provoked by the strife that broke out among the disciples about which of them would be the greatest (Lk. 22:24).

It was customary in those days that, as a guest entered a house, a servant would meet him at the entrance where his feet would be washed before entering the house. Going to an important event such as a Passover meal, the attendees would bathe before arriving, but walking through the city streets behind the horses and donkeys their feet would be dirtied; however, as Jesus and the disciples arrived at the house for Passover, there was no one to wash their feet, and none of the twelve were willing to humble themselves for this menial task. When the twelve began arguing, instead of rebuking them for their pride, Jesus simply began to demonstrate to them the humility that they should have towards one another.

Each of the disciples humbly submitted to this act of kindness by Jesus until he came to Simon Peter who protested that he would never allow Jesus to wash his feet. I am sure Peter believed this statement to resist this demonstration of servant-hood by Jesus was somehow honoring him, but Jesus responded by saying, "If I wash you not, you have no part with me" (Jn. 13:8). Peter then submits to Jesus by offering his hands and head for washing also, but Jesus assures him that if he has washed he only needs to wash his feet to be completely clean, then adds, "'you are clean, but not all of you.' For he knew who would betray Him; therefore said he, 'You are not all clean'" (Jn. 13:10,11). Jesus was speaking metaphorically here in at least two ways.

First, having been cleansed, it is only necessary to clean our feet. Our feet represent our walk, our way of life. Having been cleansed by the blood of the Lamb of God we are clean, but walking in the world, our feet may become defiled, and we may need to cleanse ourselves with the "washing of water by the word" (Eph. 5:26). Secondly, Jesus is referring to Judas who was about to betray him. All of the disciples were clean, their hearts were sincere, and they were committed to Jesus except Judas Iscariot, who had already agreed with the Jewish council to betray him. Jesus then put on his garments and reclined at the table with the disciples, teaching them that if he, being their Lord and Master, had served them, how much more so should they be willing to serve one another.

Then, Jesus institutes one of the major sacraments of the church.

"He took bread, and gave thanks, and brake it, and gave unto them, saying, 'This is my body which is given for you: this do in remembrance of me. Likewise also the cup after supper, saying, This cup is the new testament in my blood, which is shed for you'" (Lk. 22:19,20).

Remember, the Passover meal had ended. This meal included eating the lamb with "unleavened bread; and with bitter herbs" (Ex. 12:8). The evening following Passover began the seven-day Feast of

Unleavened Bread. There was to be no leaven in the Jewish houses for seven days, from the "fourteenth day of the month at evening you shall eat unleavened bread, until the one and twentieth day of the month at evening" (Ex. 12:18). Jesus and his disciples ate the roasted lamb with unleavened bread and bitter herbs as the feast required, but after the Passover meal had ended Jesus then "took bread" (Lk. 22:19). What Jesus did is not obvious in the English translations of this scripture, but in the Greek language the word for bread used here is "*artos*" or risen bread. That is bread with leaven.

Jesus and his disciples apparently ate the Passover meal during the "Day of Preparation." That was the same day (which begins in the evening) when the lamb was to be slain. After the lamb was slain, Israel was to eat the roasted lamb with unleavened bread that night. Since Jesus was the paschal lamb who would be slain at three o'clock on the day of preparation, he and his disciples actually ate the Passover meal on the day of preparation before the Feast of Unleavened Bread began. Therefore, Jesus did not violate the law regarding leaven.

Leaven, in scripture, usually references sin. That is why the eating of only unleavened bread at Passover and the following seven days during the Feast of Unleavened Bread indicates the work of the sacrificial lamb that cleanses us from sin. Paul writes to the Corinthians instructing them, "Therefore let us keep the feast, not with old leaven, neither with the leaven of malice and wickedness; but with the unleavened bread of sincerity and truth" (1 Cor. 5:8).

However, leaven can also represent the kingdom of God. Jesus said, "The kingdom of heaven is like unto leaven, which a woman took, and hid in three measures of meal, till the whole was leavened" (Mt. 13:33). After the Passover meal had ended, Jesus then took leavened or risen bread and gave thanks, and broke it, and gave it to them saying, "This is my body which is given for you: this do in remembrance of me" (Lk. 22:19).

Years later Paul, writing to the Corinthian church, instructed them that, "The cup of blessing which we bless, is it not the communion of the blood of Christ? The bread [*artos*] which we break, is it not the communion of the body of Christ? For we being many are one bread, and one body: for we are all partakers of that one bread" (1 Cor. 10:16,17).

Isn't it interesting that, after partaking of the Lamb, we become freed from sin and become partakers of the risen Body of Christ? Jesus was born in Bethlehem (House of Bread), and as he said, he is the "bread of life" (Jn. 6:48). In the Temple was the "showbread" or bread of his presence. This bread is always leavened or risen bread. The showbreads were twelve loaves baked fresh every Sabbath day and placed in the holy place in the Temple. Each of these loaves represented one of the twelve tribes of Israel, made of risen bread, and showing that the people of God would be partakers of a "risen" Savior. As Jesus said, "I am the living bread which came down from heaven: if any man eat of this bread, he shall live for ever: and the bread that I will give is my flesh, which I will give for the life of the world" (Jn. 6:51). After blessing and breaking the bread with his disciples, he took the cup, "after supper" (Lk. 22:20). The commemorative feast was over, and with the cup of wine, Jesus stated, "This cup is the new testament in my blood, which is shed for you" (Lk. 22:20).

The word transliterated into English from the Latin word "testametum" is the same word translated covenant, which references a Hebrew word meaning "to cut". A covenant was a cutting in order to shed blood. The Old Testament or Covenant is in reference to God making a covenant with Abraham.

In Genesis, chapter fifteen, God cut a covenant with Abraham. God instructed Abraham to take animals and slay them and divide them into two pieces. Then God passed through the blood of those divided animals and swore to Abraham about his "seed" or children that God would use to bless all of humanity (Gen. 15:17,18; Gen.

12:2,3). That day God made a "blood covenant" with Abraham. This was, in essence, a covenant of promise, not only to the physical descendents of Abraham who would become a great nation, but to a single seed (child) that would be born, according to the flesh by Mary who was of the seed of Abraham. Paul writes to the Galatian churches and explains to them that the "seed" promised to Abraham would bless all of humanity and that this promise was fulfilled in the birth of Jesus (Gal. 3:16).

Now Jesus was making a blood covenant with his heavenly Father. He would lay down his life (Jn. 10:18), shedding his blood and experiencing death as the righteous payment for the sin of mankind. As the sacrificial Lamb of God, Jesus fulfilled the covenant promise God made to Abraham. However, while the strength of the Old Covenant promise was dependant on Abraham's obedience (offering up his son Isaac), the strength of the New Covenant is based on the obedience of Jesus and accomplished by the shedding of his blood. The surety of the New Covenant is much better than the Old, because it is not about man's obedience but Christ's. Jesus made and fulfilled an unbreakable covenant with God, his Father, so if we are "in" Christ we are partakers of the same covenant. So Jesus can say to his disciples, this cup is the new covenant made by my blood.

BETRAYAL BY JUDAS ISCARIOT

After eating the bread and drinking from the cup, Jesus then said, "But, behold, the hand of him that [betrays] me is with me on the table" (Lk. 22:21). Jesus did not openly identify Judas as the betrayer, but when he made it known to the twelve that it was one of them, they had no idea who that one might be (Jn. 13:22). What happened next reveals the compassion Jesus had, even for the one that did betray him.

The twelve were reclining on cushions around a very low table, and while we don't know where each of the twelve were sitting, we do know that to sit on the right and left hand of Jesus was a position of great honor (Mt. 20:21). One disciple who always identifies himself as, the one Jesus loves (John) was on the right hand of Jesus, leaning against him (Jn. 13:23). Simon Peter appears to have been across the table from John and motioned to him to ask Jesus who the betrayer was (Jn. 13:24). When John asked Jesus, he replied, "It is he to whom I shall give a piece of bread when I have dipped it" (Jn. 13:26 NKJV). Jesus dipped the bread and gave it to Judas saying to him, "What you do, do quickly" (Jn. 13:27 NASB)). No one knew what Jesus meant when he said this to Judas, but they assumed that Jesus was asking Judas to go buy more provisions for the feast or to go and give something to the poor because Judas was the treasurer of the group and carried the bag of money (Jn. 13:28,29).

We learn several things about Jesus and Judas from this passage of scripture. First, Jesus gave Judas a position of honor next to him at the table. We know this because the only person Jesus could have given the bread to was the one on his immediate left-hand. Secondly, we see that Judas was the treasurer of the group. Although Jesus knew he was a thief and stole money from the bag (Jn. 12:6), Judas had the responsibility of purchasing supplies and giving to the poor which must have been a regular practice for the twelve to think that this was the reason he left the table. It was already dark when Judas left the upper room, and presumably, he headed to the Jewish council to inform them that Jesus was alone with the twelve, so they could come and arrest him.

Jesus began teaching the remaining eleven disciples as they reclined around the table. He told them that the time for his glorification had come and that, where he was going, they could not come now at that time. He gave them a new commandment to love one another as he has loved them, and he told them that the demonstration of that love would cause all to know that they were his disciples (Jn. 13:31-35).

The extent of this love would be a willingness to lay down their lives for others. With that Simon Peter said to Jesus, "Lord, why cannot I follow you now? I will lay down my life for your sake" (Jn. 13:37 NKJV). Jesus then told Peter that he was not yet willing to lay down his life. In fact, Jesus told Peter that he would deny him three times before the sun rose in the morning (Jn. 13:38).

Jesus continued teaching them about the work he was about to do in preparing a place for them in his Father's house (Jn. 14:1-3). He told them that he was the only way to the Father and that they should know that it was the Father that dwelt in him and that the Father was the one that worked through him to do the miraculous things he had done (Jn. 14:9-11). He continued to encourage them to believe in him and said that, if they would do his will, he would send them a "Comforter" to live in them. The "Comforter" is the Holy Spirit, and he would both comfort them and teach them just as Jesus did (Jn. 14:25,26). After Jesus had encouraged his disciples to be at peace even though he was about to leave them, he promised them they would see him again (Jn.14:18). He concluded this time at the table by saying to them, "But that the world may know that I love the Father; and as the Father gave me commandment, even so I do. Arise, let us go hence" (Jn. 14:31).

Leaving the upper room, Jesus and the eleven made their way through the streets of Jerusalem, and soon they crossed the Kidron valley to ascend the Mount of Olives. As they were walking together, Jesus began to instruct them regarding the power of prayer. As they passed a vineyard, Jesus used the analogy of the vine and the branches to emphasize the need to abide in him in order to bear fruit (Jn. 15:1-9).

Jesus had just demonstrated his love for the Father by arising from the table to fulfill the commandment his Father had given him (Jn. 14:31). He then emphasized to the disciples his commitment to love them and commanded them to demonstrate this same love.

Jesus further explained that his commandment to them was to love one another as he had loved them. He told them that the result of abiding in his love would be great joy (Jn. 15:11).

There are many scriptural references about the love of God even to John's declaration that "God is love" (1 Jn. 4:8,16). But this love is not limited to an emotion or tender feeling, but it is a commitment to demonstrate love for God and for others regardless of the cost to us. Laying down our lives does not always end in physical death, but it is the choice to forgo one's own comfort or convenience for the good and success of someone else.

Jesus continued exhorting the eleven that the greatest demonstration of love is expressed in a man laying down his life for his friends (Jn. 15:13) and that Jesus considered the eleven his friends, not his servants. He then warned them that the world would not accept or understand the love of God and would, therefore, reject him and all who follow him. The unbelief in the world would be met with the fact that the miraculous works Jesus did had never been done by any man before and those works give testimony of who he is. Then, once again, he promised them that he would send to them the Comforter, who is the Holy Spirit, who would testify to who Jesus is because of the miraculous works that would be done through all those who believe in Jesus (Jn. 14:12; 15:26,27).

Jesus was still walking and teaching the eleven as he was nearing the Garden of Gethsemane. John continues the record of that teaching in chapter sixteen. John chapter sixteen carries three major themes: persecution, the work of the Holy Spirit, and the power of prayer. These were the last few minutes Jesus had with his disciples before his arrest and trial, so his words for them are of upmost importance.

First, Jesus warned his disciples about offenses. This word "offended" is taken from a Greek word meaning to entrap, trip up, entice to sin or apostasy. Jesus was warning his disciples about the persecution they would face. Just being associated with Jesus would cause them to be expelled from the synagogues, slandered, and even put to death as heretics, and the perpetrators of those acts would declare that they were acting as God's agents. The pain of rejection and ridicule could cause them to draw back from the mission Jesus had given them, so Jesus said to them, "these things have I told you, that when the time shall come, [you] may remember that I told you of them…" (Jn. 16:4). When Jesus was with them, there was nothing for them to question because he would both defend them and reinforce to them who he was, but now he was about to leave them and sorrow was filling their hearts (Jn. 16:6).

It is because of these very circumstances that Jesus then began to encourage them about the work of the Holy Spirit, showing them the necessity for him to leave them so that the Holy Spirit would come to them. He explained, "It is expedient for you that I go away: for if I go not away, the Comforter will not come unto you; but if I depart, I will send him unto you" (Jn. 16:7). Jesus was anointed with the Holy Spirit and power (Acts 10:38), but he could only be in one place at a time. As long as Jesus was with the disciples, the power of God and the work of the Holy Spirit was with them. Now he was leaving them, but he was showing them that after he did he would send the Holy Spirit so that they could do the work of God through the Spirit and power of God within them (Rom. 8:11; Acts 1:8; Jn. 14:12).

Jesus described the work of the Holy Spirit in three ways: to convince and convict the world of sin, righteousness, and judgment. Sin literally means to fall short or miss the mark. People fall short of God's required perfection not only by the sinful acts they commit (idolatry, adultery, murder, falsehood, etc…) but also because of the sinful nature they possess. It is just "in" them to do wrong. The wrong deeds of mankind carry with them a punishment of death. Jesus was headed to the cross where he would suffer the punishment of death for sin for all of mankind, so the conviction the Holy Spirit brings to the world is not so much the feeling of guilt someone who does something sinful feels, but it is the conviction the Holy Spirit brings to people of their unbelief in the work of Jesus (Jn. 16:9). If sinful people turn to Jesus, he does not just forgive their sinful acts, but he gives them a new nature. Now, people have "in" them the desire to do what is right.

The Spirit also convinces people of "righteousness." Jesus, after paying the price for the sins of the world, ascended to God the Father and sits at His right hand. Jesus is righteous (the state or condition of purity, holiness, being accepted with God). The Spirit of God convinces people that Jesus is righteous and those who believe in Jesus are also righteous, not because of their deeds, but because of their faith. Righteousness is a gift received, not a state acquired (Rom. 5:17). The Holy Spirit not only convinces the unbeliever of his unbelief and need of righteousness, but the Spirit convinces the believer that he is righteous because he has received the righteous one (Jesus). It seems that the devil is always at work to try to discredit Jesus in the eyes of the world, but he also works in the lives of believers to convince them that they are unworthy and unqualified to fulfill the purpose and destiny Jesus wants for them. So the Spirit of God brings spiritual strength to the believers to see themselves as God sees them, cleansed and made righteous by the blood of Jesus and equipped and prepared for the work of God.

The third work of the Spirit Jesus described is regarding judgment, "Of judgment because the prince of this world is judged" (Jn. 16:11). The "prince of this world" is Satan or the devil. He is the prince (ruler, commander, leader, first in rank) of this world. The world is the "*kosmos*," the orderly arrangement, i.e. the way things get done. Some misunderstand, thinking the term world here is referring to the planet, but it is not. "The earth is the Lord's, and the fullness thereof; the world, and they that dwell therein" (Ps. 24:1). God is the creator of all things, but Satan has ordered the "world's system" to function by fear and tyranny. That is why we are told not to "love the world," for "If any one loves the world, the love of the Father is not in him" (1 Jn. 2:15 NKJV). Jesus identifies "the prince of this world" as the one who is coming to him, but "he has nothing in me" (Jn. 14:30). The Apostle Paul describes Satan as the "god of this world" (2 Cor. 4:4). Just as Jesus is the King of the kingdom of God, Satan is the "god" or prince of this world's system and the way it functions. Jesus came to "destroy the works of the devil" (1 Jn. 3:8), and the Spirit of God bears witness to us that the prince of the world has been judged. Believers carry the gospel of the kingdom of God to the ends of the earth by the power of the Holy Spirit, and as they do, then "the kingdoms of this world are become the kingdoms of the Lord, and of his Christ: and he shall reign for ever and ever" (Rev. 11:15).

Jesus is revealing to his disciples the many ways the Spirit of God will help them when he arrives. He will guide them into all truth; he will speak to believers what he hears and show them things to come. He will glorify Jesus, and he will take that which Jesus has, and he will show it to them that they may not walk ignorantly or in confusion but in the wisdom and understanding he will bring.

The disciples discuss among themselves about a statement Jesus made to them, "a little while, and [you] shall not see me: and again a little while and [you] shall see me" (Jn. 16:17). They were confused, and yet they were afraid to ask Jesus what he meant. Jesus knew that they wanted to ask him this question, so as they walk, he answered them with a parable about the sorrow a woman may endure in the process of childbirth, but once the baby is born it brings her great joy. "Therefore you now have sorrow," Jesus said to them, recognizing their anxiety about him leaving them, Then, he added, "but I will see you again, and your heart shall rejoice" (Jn. 16:22 NKJV). This leads us to the third major theme of chapter sixteen, the power of prayer.

Jesus explained to the eleven, "in that day," beginning the day he would see them again and the Holy Spirit would come to them, they would not ask Jesus for anything. He told them, "Whatsoever [you] shall ask the Father in my name, he will give it you" (Jn. 16:23). Jesus

Preparation for Passover

told them that up until that time they had never asked for anything in his name, but now they were to, not only ask, but also to receive so that their "joy may be full" (Jn. 15:11). These scriptures are far more powerful than most people recognize.

Before Jesus had accomplished the hard work of redemption (like the woman in labor), his disciples had always asked him for things, but now, after the work was completed, they would not ask him for anything because they will ask the Father in the authority of the name of Jesus, and what they asked would be given to them (Jn. 16:23).

Again, the English translation of these scriptures does not convey the entire idea expressed in the Greek language. In verse twenty-three the first word translated "ask," is a word meaning "to request." If we make a request of someone, we don't know what the answer might be. The disciples had often asked Jesus about things, not knowing what he might answer, questions like "Where shall we get bread in the wilderness" (Mk 8:4, my paraphrase) or "Do you want us to call fire down from heaven? (Lk. 9:54, my paraphrase). But now, they were entering into a new day and a new age where things would be done differently so Jesus said to them, "whatsoever [you] shall ask the Father in my name, he will give it you" (Jn. 16:23). This word "ask" has a different meaning. It means to command or demand something that is due. Verse twenty-four continues, "Up till now you have demanded nothing in my name: demand and you shall receive, that your joy may be full" (This is my paraphrase of this scripture). (Note: see Strong's concordance Copyright 1995, 1996 by Thomas Nelson Publishers; Greek Dictionary of the New Testament, page 78, numerical code: 4441).

Many hearing this for the first time may think this idea to be false or even blasphemous, but what Jesus was relaying to his disciples was how they were to pray in the authority of his name. They were not to make a request, asking God to do something and not knowing if it was good or bad, right or wrong, but instead they were to know the will of God because the Spirit would show them the things of God. They were to demand that God's will is done. Jesus was not saying to command God to do whatever they want, but he was trying to show them that once the Spirit of God came upon them and lived inside them, they were to follow the leading of the Holy Spirit to speak to everything and anything that was contrary to the will of God, and they were to command God's will to be done in that situation. Jesus taught them to pray to the Father, "Thy kingdom come, Thy will be done in earth, as it is in heaven" (Mt. 6:10). Praying this way is how God's will is to be accomplished in the earth. If God's will was just automatically done then why pray?

This portion of scripture is not an exhaustive study on prayer. We know there are many kinds of prayer (Eph. 6:18) and sometimes "we do not know how to pray as we ought" (Rom. 8:26). The emphasis Jesus was making here on demanding in the authority of his name shows us that he was revealing to his disciples that they would stand in his authority and call forth his will to be done so that he would be glorified and his name praised. We, most often, understand prayer to be asking or requesting of God, but the miraculous works Jesus performed were never the result of his asking the Father. He would most often say things like: "be clean" to the leper; "be opened" to the blind eyes, "go your way; your son lives" to the father, "arise" to the dead girl, "come out" to Lazarus, "be still" to the storm; "no man eat of you forever" to the fig tree. These declarations were what the disciples were to do as they were sent to the nations to declare the gospel in the authority of the name of Jesus.

Jesus warned the disciples that the hour was nearing when they would all be scattered and would leave him alone (Jn. 16:32). He also encouraged them that even though some of the things he has just shown them could disturb and trouble them, that his desire for them was to have peace, for, in spite of the trouble in the world, they could be cheerful because he had "overcome the world" (Jn. 16:33).

Preparation for Passover

John is the only gospel writer that records the prayer of Jesus in chapter seventeen. This prayer to the Father must have been done while he was still with the eleven and before he came to the Garden of Gethsemane because chapter eighteen begins with Jesus and the disciples crossing over the brook Cedron (Kedron) on his way to the garden (Jn. 18:1). Chapter seventeen is the most detailed prayer of Jesus recorded in the scriptures. In this prayer, he was revealing to his disciples things about his relationship with God the Father and Jesus' desire regarding the eleven disciples that were with him as well as the multitudes of believers that would believe on him in the ages to come (Jn. 17:20).

The things Jesus reveals as he prays:

1. The hour had come for the Father to glorify the Son that he might glorify the Father.

2. Jesus has authority over all flesh to give eternal life to those given to him by God.

3. Jesus has glorified God on earth and has finished the work he was given to do.

4. Jesus desired the glory he had with the Father to be restored as it was even before the world was.

5. Jesus manifested God's name to the men given him out of the world, and they had kept the word the Father had given them.

6. Those God gave Jesus know that he has come from God.

7. Jesus gave men the words he was given, and they received them and have known Jesus came from the Father, and they believe the Father sent him.

8. Jesus was not praying for the world but for those the Father has given him.

9. All who belong to God belong to Jesus, and all Jesus has belongs to God, and Jesus is glorified in those who belong to him.

10. Jesus was no more in the world because he was going to the Father, but the disciples were in the world, and Jesus prayed for their protection and oneness as Jesus and the Father are one.

11. Jesus kept all he had been given except the son of perdition; that the scripture would be fulfilled.

12. Jesus was speaking these things while he was in the world, and before he went to the Father so that his disciples might have his joy fulfilled in them.

13. Those who have received the word are hated by the world because they are not of the world, even as Jesus is not of the world.

14. Jesus prays that the disciples not be taken out of the world but kept from the evil in the world.

15. The disciples were sanctified through the truth and God's word is truth.

16. The disciples were sent into the world just as Jesus was sent into the world.

17. Jesus sanctified himself that his disciples might also be sanctified.

18. This prayer is not just for those disciples of that time but also for all disciples of all time.

19. The unity of Jesus and the Father would also be known and experienced by the disciples so the world would believe God sent Jesus.

20. Jesus gave his disciples the same glory God gave him so that they might be one.

21. The disciples would be made perfect in unity so that the world would know that God had sent Jesus and that God loves them just like he loves Jesus.

22. Jesus desires his disciples be with him where he is and behold the glory God gave him, for he was loved by the Father before the foundation of the world.

23. The world does not know the Father, but Jesus does, and his disciples believe that God sent Jesus.

24. Jesus declared the name of the Father to his disciples so that the love the Father has for Jesus would be in them and Jesus would be in them.

Chapter 17

The Passion of Christ

Still walking towards the garden, Jesus said to his disciples, "All of [you] shall be offended because of me this night: for it is written, I will smite the shepherd, and the sheep of the flock shall be scattered abroad" (Mt. 26:31). Peter quickly responded to Jesus by boldly declaring that even if everyone else were to deny Jesus he would never do so, but he is willing to go to prison and to death for Jesus (Mt. 26:33; Lk. 22:33). Jesus took note of Peter's words but said to him, "…today, even this night, before the rooster crows twice, you will deny Me three times" (Mk. 14:30 NKJV). Peter continued his assertion that he would never deny Jesus, and with that, all the other disciples said the same thing (Mt. 26:35; Mk. 14:31).

Luke's account, of these things give us some additional instructions that Jesus gave to his disciples. Jesus began by asking the eleven this question,

> "When I sent you without money bag, knapsack, and sandals, did you lack anything?"
>
> So they said, "Nothing."
>
> Then He said to them, "But now, he who has a money bag, let him take *it*, and likewise a knapsack; and he who has no sword, let him sell his garment and buy one. For I say to you that this which is written must still be [a]accomplished in Me: 'And He was numbered with the transgressors.' For the things concerning Me have an end." (Lk. 22:35-37 NKJV).

It appears that Jesus was doing two things here. First, he was reminding his disciples how they were cared for when he sent them out to preach and minister to the needs of the people, but now they would not be able to rely on the favor of the people to receive them, so they must take with them what they required. Secondly, Jesus was fulfilling every word of prophecy; Isaiah says the Messiah would be, "numbered with the transgressors" (Isa. 53:12). The purchasing of swords indicates the coming conflict Jesus and his disciples would face. When the disciples announced that they had two swords, Jesus replied "it is enough" (Lk. 22:38).

Crossing the brook Cedron (Kidron), Jesus and his disciples ascended the face of the Mount of Olives and came to a garden (Jn. 18:1). John makes mention that Judas was familiar with this place because Jesus went there often. As he entered the garden called Gethsemane (oil press), Jesus commanded eight of his disciples to wait for him while he took Peter, James, and John with him further into the garden (Mt. 26:36,37). Here Jesus became "exceeding sorrowful" (overcome with sorrow) and "heavy" (great distress or anguish) and asked the three to wait and pray while he went further into the garden alone. When he was alone, Jesus cried out to his Father, asking that if it were possible to "let this cup pass from me: nevertheless not as I will, but as [you] will" (Mt. 26:39).

Earlier Jesus had asked James and John if they could drink of the cup he was going to drink from (Mt. 20:22) in response to their mother's request for them to sit on the left and right hand of Jesus when he sat on the throne of his kingdom. Eating and drinking were symbols for experiencing something we take into our lives. A cup could be a cup of blessing as in the Lord's Supper or a cup of judgment as is described in Isaiah where the prophet speaks of Jerusalem drinking of the cup of God's fury (Isa. 51:17). The Book of Revelation tells us that John was told to eat the little book in the hand of the angel (Rev. 10:8-11). After he ate the book, John's belly was bitter, but in his mouth, the taste was sweet. In other words, the Word of God was good and sweet to John, but it made his belly bitter because of the prophetic judgment he would speak over peoples, nations, and kings. In the garden, Jesus expressed that the contents of the cup that was being presented to him would be difficult to swallow. It was the cup of cursing and judgment that he would receive on behalf of the whole world, resulting in much more than physical death. It would mean that he and his Father would be separated for the first time. Both man and God would reject Jesus as he carried the sin and judgment for the sin of all humanity to the cross. It is no wonder Jesus was overwhelmed with the magnitude of the things he would soon experience and sought to discover another way. But as Jesus declared earlier, he had come down from heaven, not to do his will, but the will of him who had sent him (Jn. 6:38), so now he declared again "not as I will, but as [you] will" (Mt. 26:39).

> Leaving the place of prayer, Jesus returned to Peter, James, and John and found them sleeping instead of praying. Awakening them, he warned them, saying, "Watch and pray, lest you enter into temptation" (Mt. 26:41 NKJV).

To watch is to stay awake or give their full attention to prayer in order to avoid the coming temptation. Even in Jesus' most desperate hour, he was still teaching, encouraging and protecting his chosen. He had already warned Peter of his denying him before the rooster crowed at the break of day and reassured him that, although Satan had desired to "sift him as wheat," he would be the one to "strengthen [his] brethren" (Lk. 22:32) because Jesus had prayed for him.

Jesus left them a second time to pray earnestly for the will of his Father to be done; then, returning to the three, he found them asleep again (Mt. 26:42,43). The help and support Jesus now needed would not come from those men to whom he was closest, so leaving the three, he returned to his place of prayer a third time where he was strengthened by the appearance of an angel (Lk. 22:43).

Jesus experienced such agony in this time of prayer that Luke tells us his sweat was like "great drops of blood falling down to the ground" (Lk. 22:44). He had already told Peter, James, and John, "My soul is exceeding sorrowful, even unto death" (Mt. 26:38).

I do not think that it is possible to put into words the extreme suffering in the soul of Jesus. The rupture of the capillaries in Jesus' forehead best expressed the agony he experienced as he was literally sweating blood. It seems his struggle was bringing his own will into agreement with the will of his Father. Jesus prayed for three hours, saying, repeatedly, "O my Father, if it be possible, let this cup pass from me: nevertheless not as I will, but as you wilt; O my Father, if this cup may not pass away from me, except I drink it, [your] will be done" (Mt. 26:39,42).

Once Jesus was certain and totally resigned to fulfill the will of his Father, he returned to his disciples, and yes, they were sleeping once again (Mt. 26:40). His response to them this time was, "Are you still sleeping and resting? Behold, the hour is at hand, and the Son of Man is being betrayed into the hands of sinners. Rise, let us be going.

See, My betrayer is at hand" (Mt. 26:45,46 NKJV). Just then, Judas arrived, leading the temple guards to arrest Jesus.

The purpose of the disciples being armed may be in reference to the conflict in the garden when the multitude with swords, led by Judas, arrived at the garden. One of the disciples drew a sword and cut off the ear of the servant to the high priest (Mt. 26:47-50).

Looking at all the gospels gives us a better understanding of what happened. Jesus' response to the disciple who drew the sword was, "Put up again [your] sword into his place: for all they that take the sword shall perish with the sword. [Think] that I cannot now pray to my Father, and he shall presently give me more than twelve legions of angels?" (Mt. 26:52,53).

Jesus was not powerless as he faced his betrayer and the armed guards who accompanied him. It is in John's account where we discover that Jesus led his disciples to meet those who had come to arrest him. As always, Jesus took control of the circumstance by asking, "Whom do you seek?" (Jn, 18:4). "Jesus of Nazareth," they answered, and with that, Jesus said to them, "I Am" (Jn. 18:6 CJB). What happened next shook his assailants and made it crystal clear who was in control because as soon as Jesus said I AM, they all fell backward to the ground (Jn.18:6). The awesome power that subdued Judas and those who followed him was the result of Jesus calling himself by the name of God. When Moses encountered the burning bush in the desert and subsequently talked with God, asking his name, God replied, "I AM THAT I AM" (Ex. 3:14). The I AM was really the one Judas betrayed and the one religious leaders were attempting to arrest.

As they were picking themselves up off of the ground, Jesus asked them again, "Whom do you seek"? Again, they answered, "Jesus of Nazareth". I am sure that this time they were not so arrogant, recognizing that, if Jesus did not go with them willingly, they had no power to arrest him. Jesus had already said to the Pharisees many weeks earlier that no man would take his life from him, but that he alone had power to lay it down (Jn. 10:18). He would give his life willingly. It would be his choice, not mans'.

It is in John's account where we discover that it was Simon Peter who drew the sword and cut off the ear of the high priest's servant whose name was Malchus (18:10). This may be what Isaiah prophesied about the Messiah who would be, "numbered with the transgressors" (Is. 53:12). Those disciples who stood with Jesus with swords could have been subject to arrest, but Jesus had already prayed regarding the twelve that "none of them [would be] lost, but the son of perdition; that the scripture might be fulfilled" (Jn.17:12). John gives the fulfilling of Jesus' prayer in chapter 17 as the reason Jesus told those who came to arrest him to let the disciples go free (Jn. 18:8,9).

The evident power Jesus demonstrated when those coming to arrest him fell to the ground must have convinced them that they should be content with arresting Jesus but letting the disciples go. Just before they took Jesus into custody, he turned to Malchus and healed his ear (Lk. 22:51). There is one account regarding the arrest of Jesus that is unique to Mark's gospel. Here it tells us of a certain young man that was clothed only in a linen cloth, and when Jesus was arrested, they also laid hands on this young man who, "left the linen cloth, and fled from them naked" (Mk. 14:52). The question is, "Who was this young man?"

If we follow the events of that night, we remember that the twelve disciples met in an upper room in the city of Jerusalem where they ate the Passover meal with Jesus (Mk. 14:13-15). We do not know for certain where this upper room was, except that it was in Jerusalem. If we look at other references to upper rooms in the city, we find that the disciples and the brothers of Jesus with the women and Mary the mother of Jesus met in an upper room (Acts 1:13,14). Later on we see one of the leading apostles was a man named Barnabas, whose sister Mary lived in a house in Jerusalem with her son Mark. When Barnabas and Paul embarked on their first missionary journey to Galatia, they took Mark with them, but he did not complete the mission, and leaving them, he returned home to his mother's house in Jerusalem. It was after this that Barnabas wanted to take Mark with him and Paul on their second missionary trip, but Paul refused to take Mark. Paul's refusal caused a division that resulted in Barnabas taking Mark with him and Paul taking Silas and going a different way (Acts 15:37-39). Many years later, Paul wrote from prison in Rome, and Mark was then with him (Col. 4:10). It was this John Mark who wrote the Gospel of Mark where this story about the young man in the linen cloth is mentioned. John Mark was apparently much younger than the disciples of Jesus, but his mother and Uncle Barnabas were very active in the early church in Jerusalem. When Peter was let out of prison by an angel the church was gathered together to pray for him at Mary's house, the mother of John Mark (Acts 12:12). We see that Mary's house was a meeting place for the early church. Since Mark is the only gospel writer who adds this story about the young man who was with Judas and the angry multitude when Jesus was arrested, it has been surmised that the upper room where Jesus and his disciples ate the Passover meal may have been at Mary's house. That night, after Judas left Jesus, he went to the chief priests to lead them to where Jesus was alone with the twelve. Judas would not have known that Jesus and the others had left the upper room and gone to Gethsemane, so he would have returned to where he last saw Jesus. Judas was, most likely familiar to Mary and Mark and upon his returning, found the room empty, possibly discovering from Mary or Mark that Jesus and the others had left for Gethsemane. We already know that Judas was familiar with the place because Jesus often went there, and it could be that Mark tagged along to see what was happening, having no idea that Judas was bringing this mob to arrest Jesus. Could this be why Mark mentions that "there followed him a certain young man, having a linen cloth cast about his naked body; and the young men laid hold on him: and he left the linen cloth, and fled from them naked" (Mk. 14:51,52)? There is no definitive proof that this young man was John Mark, but it is interesting that he was the one who included this event in his gospel.

The Trial of Jesus

Leading him away from the garden, the multitude took Jesus to the house of Annas, the father-in-law to Caiaphas who was the high priest that same year (Jn. 18:13). The reason Jesus was first taken to the house of Annas was probably to give the Sanhedrin time to assemble the council. Remember it was very early in the morning before sun-up, and every council member would have been asleep in their beds when Jesus was arrested. I am sure that not all the seventy-member council was assembled because Nicodemus and Joseph of Arimathaea were favorable to Jesus (Jn. 19:38,39).

Once a quorum of council members was assembled, Jesus was taken to the palace of the high priest (Jn. 18:24). John's gospel shows us what else was happening at the same time that Jesus was before the council. We see from Mark's account that, when Jesus was bound, all his disciples fled (Mk. 14:50), but once Jesus was sent from the house of Annas to the high priest, John and Peter followed this procession a far off. We have no scriptures that tell us why, but apparently John knew the high priest and was allowed to enter the palace (Jn. 18:15,16). Having been granted access to the court, John* then stepped outside the door and brought Peter into the court where Jesus had been taken. Here, the damsel who kept the door identified Peter as a disciple of Jesus (Jn. 18:17). Peter immediately denied it. Inside the courtyard, Peter warmed himself by a fire of coals where both servants and officers stood. One of them said to Peter, "Art not [you] also one of his disciples?" (Jn. 18:25). Again, Peter denies his

---

*[Although John is not identified by name, we learn from many places in his gospel that he is the "other" disciple or "the one whom Jesus loved." (Jn. 1:35,37-40; 13:23; 18:15; 21:20-24) John seldom identifies himself by name.]

relationship with Jesus. After that, a relative of the man whose ear Peter cut off in the garden said to Peter, "Did not I see you in the garden with him? (Jn. 18:26). Once again Peter denied Jesus (Jn. 18:27).

Both in Luke's gospel and John's record, Peter's denial has a gentler tone than it does in the books of Matthew and Mark. Both Matthew and Mark tell us that Peter began to curse and to swear, declaring that he does not know the man (Mt. 26:74; Mk. 14:71). At this moment the rooster crowed for a second time, and Jesus turned to look at Peter, and "…Peter remembered the word of the Lord, how he had said unto him, Before the cock crow, you shall deny me [three times]. And Peter went out and wept bitterly" (Lk. 22:61,62).

Jesus stood before Caiaphas the high priest and the council of scribes and elders as they sought for false witnesses against him, but they could find none. They repeatedly asked him questions, but Jesus refused to answer until the high priest turned to Jesus and said to him, "I adjure [you] by the living God, that [you] tell us whether [you] be the Christ, the Son of God" (Mt. 26:63). Jesus answered and said to him, "It is as you said. Nevertheless, I say to you, hereafter you will see the Son of Man sitting at the right hand of the Power, and coming on the clouds of heaven" (Mt. 26:64 NKJV). When Caiaphas heard Jesus speak these words, he tore his clothes and declared Jesus guilty of blasphemy (Mt.26:65).

The high priest, tearing his clothes, was just one of the many unlawful things which were done at Jesus' trial. Under the Law of Moses, it was forbidden for the high priest to tear his priestly robe (Lev. 21:10), for he was a representative of Christ and his robe was a whole piece representing the unity of the nation of Israel. The tearing of the garment representing the dividing of the kingdom is seen when the prophet Ahijah tore his garment into twelve pieces and gave ten of them to Jeroboam (1 Kings 11:29-31) and said to him, "…thus saith the Lord, the God of Israel, Behold, I will rend the kingdom out of the hand of Solomon, and will give ten tribes to thee…" (1 Kings 11:31). The unlawful tearing of the high priests' robe indicated the tearing away of the kingdom from these wicked religious leaders (Mt. 21:43).

The whole council declared Jesus guilty of blasphemy and deserving of death. They then began to spit in his face and beat him and mock him (Mt. 26:66-68). Binding him, they led him away to Pontius Pilate the Roman governor.

Another of Jesus' disciples who had watched this mock trial and conviction was Judas Iscariot. What his preconceived notions were, we do not know, but once he saw that Jesus had been condemned to death, he repented and brought the money earned through his betrayal back to the chief priests and elders who had hired him for thirty pieces of silver (Mt. 27:1-3). Maybe Judas had not expected Jesus to be condemned to death. He might have expected a different outcome that would have been less severe. Regardless of his expectations, when he heard the sentence of death, he repented and attempted to return the 30 pieces of silver, possibly hoping for the charges against Jesus to be dropped or lessened, but his repentance was only met with ridicule by the chief priests and elders. Judas told them, "I have sinned by betraying a man who has never done anything wrong," but they replied, "So what? That's your problem," (Mt. 27:4 CEV). Judas, overcome with guilt, threw down the silver coins and went out and hung himself. Judas' tragic end was prophesied by David and recognized by Jesus (Ps. 109:8; Jn. 17:12).

Picking up the silver pieces from the Temple floor, the Jewish council determined that this blood money should not be put into the treasury, so they used it to purchase a potter's field to bury strangers. Here, these "experts of the law" did not recognize their actions were fulfilling the prophetic word of Zechariah, who may have been partially quoting Jeremiah the prophet (Mt. 27:6-10; Zech. 11:12,13; Jer. 18:2-12, 19:1-15).

Jesus was taken to the hall of judgment or the palace of the Roman governor Pontius Pilate very early in the morning. The multitude that led him to the palace refused to enter requiring Pilate to come out to them. Since it was unlawful for a Jew to enter the house of a Gentile and it was the day of preparation when they would sacrifice the Passover lamb, the Jews would not enter under the governor's roof.

Pilate, having come out to them, asked, "What accusation bring [you] against this man?" (Jn. 18:29). At first, they were hesitant to answer because they knew that Pilate would not care about their accusations of blasphemy, so they just said he was a criminal. Pilate's response to them was simply, "take him and judge him according to your law". They answered him with a comment, "It is not lawful for us to put any man to death" (Jn. 18:31). Although the Jewish council could condemn one to death according to the Law of Moses, they were not to fulfill that judgment without the approval of the Romans.

Seeking a death sentence, they brought accusations against Jesus that would solicit the participation of the Romans, "We found this fellow perverting the nation, and forbidding to give tribute to Caesar, saying that he himself is Christ a King" (Lk. 23:2). Of course, this was a false accusation, for days earlier, the Jews had tried to get Jesus to say something against Caesar or paying taxes, but he would not do so (Lk. 20:25). Pilate entered the judgment hall where Jesus stood and said to him, "Are You the king of the Jews?" Jesus responded, "It is as you say" (Lk. 23:3 NKJV). Pilate was beginning to recognize that these charges they were bringing against Jesus were false, so he again went outside and said to them, "I find no fault in this man" (Lk. 23:4). The Jewish leaders immediately intensified their condemnation of Jesus saying he stirred up the people and spread his ideas among all the Jews all the way up into Galilee. Now when Pilate heard that Jesus was from Galilee, which was king Herod's jurisdiction and knowing that Herod was in town because of the feast day, Pilate instructed them to go to Herod (Lk. 23:6,7). I am sure that Pilate was glad to have Herod make the ruling regarding Jesus. He must have returned to his living quarters relieved.

King Herod had heard many things about Jesus and the miracles he had performed and was hoping to see him do some sort of a miracle in his presence (Lk. 23:8). The chief priests and scribes were vehemently accusing Jesus, and Herod, asking Jesus many things, was amazed that Jesus refused to speak. Herod and his soldiers treated Jesus with contempt and mocked him putting a gorgeous robe around him and sent him back to Pilate. (Lk. 23:10,11).

Once again Jesus and the chief priests stood before Pilate who explained to them that neither he nor Herod found in Jesus anything worthy of death, but to satisfy them Pilate would chastise him and release him according to the law that required him to release one prisoner on the feast day (Lk. 23:17). The loud cries of the Jewish leaders strongly protested the release of Jesus and provoked Pilate to give them a choice of which prisoner they would have him release to them.

Barabbas was a well-known criminal who was in prison for insurrection and murder (Mk. 15:7). Pilate knew that the Jews had accused Jesus out of envy (Mt. 27:18), and I suppose that, when given a choice, Pilate thought they would agree that Jesus should be released instead of a murderer. "But the chief priests moved the people, that he should rather release Barabbas unto them" (Mk. 15:11). Pilate then asked them, "What will [you] then that I shall do unto him whom [you] call the King of the Jews?" The overwhelming cry from this mob was "Crucify him" (Mk. 15:13). Again Pilate said unto them, "Why, what evil [has] he done? And they cried out the more exceedingly, Crucify him" (Mk. 15:14).

John's gospel tells us that at this point Pilate again said to the crowd, "I find no fault in him" (Jn. 19:6). Then, the real reason that they wanted Jesus to die was revealed. The crowd replied, "We have a law, and by our law he ought to die, because he made himself the Son of God. When Pilate therefore heard that saying, he was the more afraid" (Jn.19:7,8).

Pilate had already attempted to release Jesus three different times (Lk. 23:22) and failed, but now, knowing that Jesus had declared himself to be the Son of God, Pilate became very fearful. He, most likely, held the belief that sometimes the Roman gods would come to earth and appear as men, testing them concerning their loyalty. If Jesus truly was the Son of God, Pilate was afraid to condemn him and fall under the judgment of the gods. He returned to the hall and sat down on the judgment seat just as a messenger came with an urgent message from Pilate's wife: "Have nothing to do with that just man: for I have suffered many things this day in a dream because of him" (Mt. 27:19).

Remember it was very early in the morning while Pilate's wife was still sleeping. She dreamt about the man Pilate was about to bring judgment against. This dream was apparently troubling to Pilate's wife, causing her such concern that she felt it necessary to inform her husband. Now, Pilate was seeking any possible means to release Jesus. He returned to the crowd outside of the judgment hall and again sought to release Jesus, but the Jews cried out, saying, "If [you] let this man go, [you] are not Caesar's friend: whosoever makes himself a king [speaks] against Caesar" (Jn. 19:12).

This threat by the crowd was serious. There are various Roman historians who have written about Pilate and how he was sent to Judea because he had already fallen out of favor with Caesar. If the Jewish leaders got word to Caesar, claiming Pilate had released a man accused of treason against Rome, Pilate could lose his life. Therefore, "When Pilate saw that he could prevail nothing, but that rather a tumult was made, he took water, and washed his hands before the multitude, saying, I am innocent of the blood of this just person: see ye to it." (Mt. 27:24) The response of the people to Pilate was,

"His blood be on us, and on our children" (Mt. 27:25). Truly, the blood of Jesus would be shed. God's purpose was the forgiveness and deliverance from judgment, but these people pronounced a curse of judgment upon themselves and their children, a curse, which would be carried out forty years later when the Roman general Titus would march on the city, destroying the people and the Temple.

Jesus was then taken into the judgment hall where he was scourged with a leather whip made with several thongs each having a piece of bone or metal to strip the skin off the back. The Jewish historian Josephus wrote that some of these beatings were so severe the person's entrails could be seen.

Some have suggested that Jesus was beaten with thirty-nine stripes, which was customary for the Jews who guarded against breaking the law that limited scourging to forty stripes. (Paul makes mention that he had been beaten five times with thirty-nine stripes 2 Cor. 11:24). But Jesus was not beaten by the Jews, but by the Romans who had no limits to the number of stripes laid on a man's back. The terrible beating Jesus received coupled with the crown of thorns beaten into his skull with a reed fulfilled the scriptures that declared, "Just as many were appalled at him – his appearance was so disfigured that he did not look like a man, and his form was disfigured more than any other person" (Isa. 52:14 EHV).

One last time, after having him scourged, Pilate brought Jesus, clothed in a purple robe with the crown of thorns still on his head before the crowd and said to them, "Behold the man!" (Jn. 19:5). Maybe Pilate made sure the beating was so severe he could solicit pity from the crowd to release Jesus. However, once again, his attempt failed, and they demanded his crucifixion.

THE PASSION OF CHRIST

CRUCIFIXION

After reading the record of the crucifixion in all four gospels, it would appear that Jesus was led from the judgment hall to the place of execution called Golgotha or "the place of the skull," so named for the unusual indentations on the hillside that, from a distance, cause this hill to have the appearance of a human skull. The location of this place of execution was just outside the gates of the city. Jesus was initially carrying the transverse beam of the cross, but apparently, because of his weakened condition, the Roman soldiers conscripted a man named Simon a Cyrenian to carry it (Mk. 15:21).

We don't know anything about this man apart from his name, Simon and the names of his children, Alexander and Rufus. The Cyrenians had their own synagogue in the city of Jerusalem (Acts 6:9) and apparently Simon and his sons had come for the Feast of Passover. Mark is the only gospel writer to include the names of his sons who must have been well known to his Roman readers.

After ascending the hillside Jesus was offered a cup of wine mingled with myrrh, an opiate to dull the pain. Upon tasting it, Jesus refused. After stretching out his arms on the transverse, they nailed him through the wrists to the beam and hoisted it to its place on the upright beam and nailed his feet in place. Through the excruciating pain, Jesus prayed, "Father, forgive them; for they know not what they do" (Lk. 23:34).

Pilate wrote a title in Greek, Hebrew, and Latin and put it on the cross: JESUS CHRIST OF NAZARETH THE KING OF THE JEWS (Jn. 19:19). Luke records these words written on the cross: "THIS IS THE KING OF THE JEWS" (23:38). When the Jewish leaders read the placard, they complained to Pilate, wanting the title changed, but he told them, "What I have written I have written" (Jn. 19:22). Pilate had not succeeded in any arguments with the Jews that day, and he was not about to back down from this assertion of his authority. Legally, those accused of a capital offense would have been paraded through the city streets with a placard listing their crimes in order to solicit any witnesses either for or against the accused. This legal requirement was not fulfilled when it came to the trial of Jesus. Listing the offender's crimes, a placard would be nailed to the cross of the condemned. Jesus' only crime was being the "King of the Jews."

It was nine o'clock in the morning when Jesus was crucified, and with him, two others were condemned to die for their crimes. Those who were crucified were stripped naked, and the soldiers divided their clothing among themselves except for the long-sleeved seamless robe worn by Jesus. For this they cast lots to see which one of them would win the prize of this valuable garment (Jn. 19:23,24). As the day progressed, the chief priests, scribes, and elders took turns mocking and ridiculing Jesus, saying, "He saved others; himself he cannot save. If he be the King of Israel, let him now come down from the cross, and we will believe him" (Mt. 27:42). "And they that passed by railed on him, wagging their heads, and saying, Ah [you] that [destroy] the temple, and [build] it in three days, save [yourself], and come down from the cross" (Mk. 15:29,30). All of these events at the cross were prophesied centuries before in the 22nd Psalm:

- "My God, my God why have you forsaken me?" (22:1)

- "All they that see me laugh me to scorn: they shoot out the lip, they shake the head, saying, He trusted on the Lord that he would deliver him: let him deliver him, seeing he delighted in him" (22:7.8)

- "I am poured out like water, and all my bones are out of joint: my heart is like wax; it is melted in the midst of my bowels." (22:14)

- "My strength is dried up like a potsherd; and my tongue cleaves to my jaws; and [you] have bought me into the dust of death." (22:15)

- "…they pierced my hands and my feet" (22:16)

- "They part my garments among them, and cast lots upon my vesture" (22:18)

- "They shall come and shall declare his righteousness unto a people that shall be born, that it is finished" (22:31)

All that had been prophesied about the Messiah, the suffering he would endure and the events at the cross were perfectly fulfilled. Jesus said, "Think not that I am come to destroy the law, or the prophets: I am not come to destroy, but to fulfill" (Mt. 5:17).

During the course of the day, one of the criminals crucified with Jesus called upon him saying, "Lord, remember me when you come into your kingdom." Jesus responded by saying, "Today shall you be with me in paradise" (Lk. 23:43 NKJV).

At noon something strange happened. Suddenly, there was a darkness over all the land until three o'clock in the afternoon (Mt. 27:45). This darkness is not explained. Three hours was far too long for an eclipse to have occurred, and there was no indication of dark clouds or a storm. Luke writes that the sun was darkened (Lk. 23:45).

There is no record of any of the events during those dark hours, but at three o'clock, Jesus said, "I thirst" (Jn. 19:28). After being presented with vinegar instead of water, Jesus cries with a loud voice, "Eli, Eli, lama sabach thani" which is interpreted, My God, my God, why have you forsaken me?" (Mt. 27:46). These words are followed with Jesus declaring, "It is finished" (Jn. 19:30) and "Father, into your hands I commend my spirit" (Lk. 23:46). The centurion who was overseeing the executions when he heard Jesus cry with a loud voice said, "Truly this man was the Son of God" (Mk. 15:39).

Crucifixion is a torturous execution that ends in suffocation. Because of the position of the arms holding the weight of the sufferer, breathing is nearly impossible without pushing the full weight of the body upward by the feet, which are nailed to the upright. This motion sends excruciating pain through the body as spasms occur each time the sufferer lifts himself upward to get a breathe of air. Eventually, the bodies become so weak that the sufferers can no longer lift themselves up and soon succumb to suffocation. When Jesus, "cried with a loud voice" (Mk. 15:37), he, obviously was not unable to get his breath. The centurion recognized that Jesus had not died as the result of crucifixion.

Jesus knew of the suffering he would face as well as the rejection by man and God. His torment in the Garden, as he prayed, was induced by the fact that he and his Father would be separated. He would be despised and rejected. It was at the three o'clock hour that God the Father had to reject His Son who had now become sin for us (2 Cor. 5:21).

This work of Jesus is foreshadowed in the sacrifices required by the Law of Moses on the Day of Atonement. Only once a year could the high priest enter beyond the veil into the most holy place where were the Ark of the Covenant and the mercy seat of God (Lev. 16:5-22). After the high priest offered a bullock for himself, he would take two goats and present them before the Lord at the door of the tabernacle. He would then cast lots to determine which goat would be for the Lord and which would be the scapegoat. The Lord's goat would be killed for the people, and the high priest would bring its blood within the veil and sprinkle the blood upon the mercy seat in the most holy place. The scapegoat would then be presented alive before the high priest, who would lay both hands upon the head of the goat and confess over it all the iniquities of the people and all their transgressions and sins, putting them upon the head of the goat. Then, the goat would be sent away into the wilderness.

The Day of Atonement and these two goats perfectly depicted the work of Jesus as our High Priest. Jesus was the Lamb of God. He was slain and his blood was shed. As our High Priest, he entered into

Heaven with his own blood and presented it upon the true mercy seat, which is the throne of God (Heb. 9:11-14). He also bore our iniquities, transgressions, and sins as the scapegoat. According to Isaiah, "Surely, he has borne our grief, and carried our sorrows"(53:4); Later he writes that "the Lord has laid on him the iniquity of us all" (53:6); adding "for he shall bear their iniquities" (53:11) and later announcing that "he bore the sin of many" (53:12). Paul tells us in the New Testament, "Now that he ascended, what is it but that he also descended first into the lower parts of the earth?" (Eph. 4:9). Jesus, as the scapegoat, carried away our sins.

On the cross Jesus was made accursed for us. The spiritual law of sin and death brought a curse upon all those who sinned. The curse of sin was death, and because everyone has sinned, the curse of death has been passed down from Adam upon us all. But Jesus took our place and paid the price for our sin, redeeming us from the curse of the law. Jesus as the promised "seed of Abraham" (Gal. 3:16) would accomplish God's promise to Abraham, bringing God's blessings upon "all the families of the earth" (Gen. 12:1-3). Redeeming all humanity from the curse of death, Jesus restored to man the inheritance God had determined for Adam and swore to Abraham. Now, by faith in Jesus Christ, we become children of God and heirs to all of God's promises (Gal. 3:13-29).

The final words of Jesus upon the cross were, "it is finished" (Jn. 19:30) and "Father, into your hands I commend my spirit" (Lk. 23:46). The work Jesus had come to do was completed. The price for the sins of humanity was paid in full, and now Jesus was committing his spirit into the hands of his Father.

As Jesus died, the veil of the Temple is torn from top to bottom (Mk. 15:38). The sin that had separated man from God was paid for, and God himself tore the veil that separated man from the most holy place of God's presence.

According to Alfred Edersheim (The Life and Times of Jesus the Messiah, page 894), the veil was sixty feet long, thirty feet wide, and as thick as the palm of a hand (about four inches). A tremendous force was required to tear such a veil, and it was torn from the top down, not the bottom up. It was a work of God, not of man. The way into the presence of God was now made available through the blood of Jesus, and we can come boldly to the throne of grace (Heb. 4:16).

At three o'clock in the afternoon, Jesus died, and because it was the day of preparation, the Jews asked Pilate that the legs of those crucified be broken so they would die quickly and their bodies could be taken off the cross before sundown because it was a "high day" (Jn. 19:31).

On what day of the week these things occurred has been disputed for centuries. John's gospel says that "it was the preparation" (19:31), so the Jews did not want the bodies of those crucified to remain on the cross on the Sabbath day, which would begin at sundown, but this day was called a "high" day. Was this the beginning of the weekly Sabbath (Saturday) or because it is called the day of preparation, was John referring to the beginning of a feast day? The Passover lamb was slain on this day, and then, the Passover meal was eaten after sundown, which was the beginning of the following day. Jesus said that the only sign that would be given to that generation would be the sign of Jonah, and as Jonah spent three days and three nights in the belly of the great fish, so the Son of man would spend three days and nights in the heart of the earth (Mt. 12:40). This analogy presents the question of whether Jesus meant three complete days and three complete nights or whether he counted days and nights as any part of a day or night. This seems to be true in some references. Also, the women went to purchase the spices for embalming the body of Jesus. They could not have done so on the Sabbath day, so the specific day may not be obvious. However, we know that the request of the Jews was granted, and the soldiers came to break the legs of those who were crucified. When they came to Jesus, the soldiers determined that he was already dead, and instead of breaking his legs, they pierced his side. This may seem like a small thing, but even this event was the fulfillment of scripture as Psalms 34:20 declares, "He keeps all his bones: not one of them is broken" and Zechariah writes, "...they shall look upon me whom they have pierced...." (12:10).

After Jesus died, Joseph of Arimathaea went to Pilate and requested his body. As Joseph of Arimathaea took Jesus' body off the cross, Nicodemus brought a mixture of myrrh and aloes, about one-hundred pounds in weight, and together these two men wound the linen cloth that had been soaked in these spices about the body of Jesus as was the custom of the Jews (Jn. 19:38-40). Jesus' body was then placed in a garden tomb not far from Golgotha.

Christ Descent into Hades

Hades was the place of the dead and was divided by a chasm separating the righteous dead from the wicked dead (Lk. 16:22-31). Having received the sins of all mankind, Jesus died physically, but also spiritually. Spiritual death is separation from God, and Jesus bore our sin and its judgment as he descended into the place of the disobedient dead (Eph, 4:9; 1 Pet. 3:18-20). At some time during the course of these three days, Jesus was born again by the Spirit of God as the "first born from the dead" (Col. 1:18). As the "firstborn of many brethren" (Rom. 8:29), Jesus preached to the disobedient spirits in prison. Jesus had said to the penitent thief on the cross," I say unto [you] today [you shall] be with me in paradise" (Lk. 23:43). Was Jesus saying to the man, "I say unto you that today you shall be with me in paradise" or did he mean "I say unto you, today, that you shall be with me in paradise"? The first sentence identifies "today" as the day he would be with Jesus in paradise, and the second sentence simply says that the man will be with Jesus in paradise at some unspecified future time – not necessarily that specific day. We may not need to understand some of these things, but what is important is that, sometime before his resurrection, Jesus crossed over that great chasm to the place of the righteous dead, who were waiting for his arrival. Until Jesus had completed the work of redemption Abraham, Moses, David, and all the Old Testament saints were at rest in paradise, but they were unable to enter heaven until the sacrifice for sins had been accomplished. Now, Jesus could lead those multitudes of captives in paradise to heaven as he "ascended up far above all heavens, that he might fill all things" (Eph. 4:10).

Another of Jesus' victories is described as possessing the keys of hell and of death (Rev. 1:18). There have been countless sermons preached and books written that indicate that Jesus went down to hell, defeated the devil and took from him the keys of hell and death. The assumption is that hell is where the devil rules and reigns and that his kingdom of darkness and his throne are in the midst of hell, but that is not at all what the Bible describes. Satan has never been in hell. Hell is not his realm of dominion or the headquarters of his operations; it is a prison house for the wicked awaiting the final judgment. The devil is the "god of this world," (2 Cor. 4:4) the "prince and the [authority] of the air, the spirit that now [works] in the children of disobedience" (Eph. 2:2). He is among those that are described as the enemies of man and the unseen rulers we wrestle against (Eph. 6:12). He and his angels will one day be cast into the lake of fire with death and hell (Rev. 20:10,14).

Keys are representative of authority. Jesus told Peter, then all of his disciples, "And I will give unto you the keys of the kingdom of heaven: and whatever you bind on earth will be bound in heaven, and whatever you loose on earth will be loosed in heaven" (Mt. 16:19 NKJV). Physical keys give one the authority to lock out or open up to permit or to refuse access to. The keys Jesus acquired and then gave to believers are spiritual in nature. These keys of spiritual authority allow believers to function in the kingdom of God. The keys of hell and death speak of the undeniable authority Jesus has because he destroyed the works of the devil (1 Jn. 3:8) and he delivered those who through the fear of death were in bondage by destroying "him that had the power of death,... the devil" (Heb. 2:14,15). Jesus defeated the devil, death, and hell, and he can prove it because he holds the keys. Hell could not keep him, death could not hold him in the grave, and the devil is forever under his feet.

Chapter 18

The Resurrection

The multitude Jesus led out of the place of paradise were now given access to heaven, but some of them returned to their bodies and came out of the graves at the resurrection of Christ. This event is only described in the gospel of Matthew. "And the graves were opened; and many bodies of the saints which slept arose, and came out of the graves after his resurrection, and went into the holy city, and appeared unto many" (Mt. 27:52,53). This may seem remarkable and present the question of why those on their way to heaven would experience a physical resurrection.

We know that "many…came out of the graves" but not all. When Peter preached to the multitudes on the Day of Pentecost, he made mention of David's sepulcher, "Men and brethren, let me freely speak unto you of the patriarch David, that he is both dead and buried, and his sepulcher is with us unto this day" (Acts 2:29). Obviously, David was not one of those who were resurrected. So who were these many who came out of the graves and walked through the streets of Jerusalem?

While there is no chapter or verse we can turn to for this information, there is a logical answer. If David, Abraham, or Moses had been resurrected and walked through the streets, no one would recognize them or believe that they were who they said they were. However, if Uncle Bob passed away a few weeks ago, and you attended his funeral and knew he was dead, and then there was a knock on your door, and you opened it to see Uncle Bob in the flesh, then Uncle Bob would be a powerful witness to the Lordship of Jesus and the resurrection of the dead. I believe that the "Uncle Bobs" were the ones who came out of the graves to bear witness of Jesus before they ascended into heaven.

It was early in the morning before the rising of the sun that Mary of Magdala, Mary the mother of Jesus, and Salome arrived at the tomb (Mk. 16:1,2). They had discussed how the large stone that covered the entrance of the tomb could be rolled away so they could enter the tomb and finish anointing of the body of Jesus with sweet spices. When they arrived, they were surprised to see the stone had already been rolled away, so they entered the tomb only to find a man in a long white garment sitting in the tomb. He informed them that Jesus had risen and that they were to go and tell his disciples and Peter that he would meet them in Galilee as he had instructed them. Apparently, Mary the mother of Jesus and Salome were afraid and did not tell anyone what they saw after they left the tomb (Mk. 16:5-8). Mary of Magdala ran to find his disciples. She first came to Peter and John and told them what she had seen. They both ran to the tomb, and John writes that he out-ran Peter (Jn.20:4). Without going inside, John saw the empty grave clothes from the entrance. Peter soon arrived and entered the empty tomb, and John joined him inside. John's gospel says that both men saw the empty tomb, but John believed. Then, they both returned to their homes (Jn. 20:1-9).

Mary returned to the tomb, weeping as she looked inside, and this time, she saw two angels sitting at the head and foot of where Jesus' body had lain. When they questioned her as to why she was weeping she answered, "Because they have taken away my Lord, and I know not where they have laid him" (Jn. 20:13). Mary did not yet understand that Jesus had been resurrected from the dead. Turning from the tomb, Mary saw Jesus standing before her but did not recognize him through her tears. When he addressed her, she immediately recognized him. Jesus instructed her not to detain him, for he had not yet ascended to his Father since rising from the dead.

Some translations say "Touch me not" which would seem to imply that her touch would some how contaminate Jesus, but the word here primarily means not to adhere or cling to. Matthew's gospel tells us that at some point Mary the mother of Jesus was with Mary of Magdala and that they "held him by the feet, and worshipped him" (Mt. 28:9). Jesus must have simply meant, "Do not detain me because I am about to ascend to my Father."

Jesus instructed them, as the angel had, to go and tell his disciples that he would meet them in Galilee. It was Mary of Magdala, Joanna, Mary the mother of Jesus, and other women who went and told these things to his disciples, but "their words seemed to them as idle tales, and they believed them not" (Lk. 24:10,11).

Luke's gospel gives us a detailed accounting of two disciples named Simon and Cleopas that traveled from Jerusalem to Emmaus the day of Jesus' resurrection. We have no information about these two men. They were not counted among the twelve disciples but were obviously acquainted with them. As they were walking together, they began discussing the events of the past several days regarding Jesus, and as they talked, Jesus joined them, listening to their conversation.

Mark explains that these two men did not recognize Jesus because "he appeared in another form" (Mk. 16:12). One of the amazing things about the resurrected body of Jesus was that he could change his appearance and appear and disappear from view (Lk. 24:31,36).

Jesus asked them about what they were discussing and the reason they seemed so sad (Lk. 24:17). Cleopas began to explain to him that a man named Jesus did many wonders among the people, but the chief priests and rulers condemned him to death and crucified him. He said they had hoped that he was the Messiah and would redeem Israel, but he died three days earlier. He also mentioned that some of the women who were of their company had gone to his tomb and found it empty and saw a vision of angels who said he was alive. Cleopas then mentioned that some of Jesus' disciples went to the tomb and found it empty, but they did not find him. About this time, Jesus spoke up and admonished them for their unbelief and began to explain the scriptures that speak of him.

As they had reached their destination and turned towards the village, Jesus continued on the road. Then, these two men invited Jesus to go with them that they might eat together. At the table, Jesus took some bread and broke it, blessed it, and gave it to them, and disappeared from their sight (Lk. 24:30). Suddenly their eyes were opened to understand that their mysterious guest was the Lord, and they quickly returned to Jerusalem to find his disciples.

Entering the upper room in Jerusalem where ten of the eleven disciples had gathered, Simon and Cleopas excitedly began to tell them that they had seen Jesus. As they spoke, Jesus appeared in the room with them and said, "Peace be unto you" (Lk. 24:36). His sudden appearance caused them to be terrified, believing they were seeing a ghost (Lk. 24:37). Jesus then assured them that it really was he standing before them and showed them the marks of crucifixion in his hands and feet (Lk. 24:38-40).

The Resurrection

There are many things we can learn from this encounter with Jesus and the two on the road to Emmaus. This was the first day of resurrection. Jesus had experienced the greatest victory of all time. He endured the cross, the curse, and defeated death. Behind him was the pain and suffering, and he now had accomplished everything his Father had sent him to do, but instead of surrounding himself with his closest friends or family, Jesus spent considerable time with two guys that were talking about him as they walked. Twice, the women who first saw the angel and then the Lord were told to tell his disciples to go to Galilee where he would meet them. Jesus did not first go to them but to two men who were confused about the events of the past several days and were sincerely looking for answers. They were not his brethren or his primary disciples, but the resurrected Christ was content to eat with these men before appearing to the twelve.

In the upper room with Cleopas, Simon, and the ten who had gathered together, Jesus ate some broiled fish and honeycomb. In John's account, we discover the response of Thomas to the news that they had seen Jesus. He had not been with the other disciples when Jesus first appeared to them. Thomas announced, "Except I shall see in his hands the print of the nails, and put my finger into the print of the nails, and thrust my hand into his side, I will not believe" (Jn. 20:25). Eight days later, when they were all gathered together again, and Thomas was with them, Jesus suddenly appeared in the room and addressed Thomas by instructing him to touch the wounds in Jesus' hands and side. Thomas had not seen Jesus eight days earlier, but Jesus had heard every word he had spoken. Thomas then believed (Jn. 20:26-28).

Jesus continued to reveal himself to his disciples over a period of forty days before he ascended into heaven (Acts 1:3). One of the most detailed exchanges between Jesus and his disciples was at the Sea of Galilee. It was sometime after the meeting with Thomas that Peter announces that he was going to go fishing. Six of the others join him at the Sea of Galilee. This was not a casual decision. The distance from Jerusalem to Galilee was about sixty miles so not all of the disciples decided to go with Peter. After fishing all night and catching nothing, they turned the boat towards the shore, and as they got closer, they saw someone in the dim light of the new day. Jesus shouted, "Friends, have you caught anything?" "No!" they answered (Jn. 21:5 CEV). "Cast the net on the right side of the [boat], and [you] shall find" (Jn.21:6). When they cast their net, they were not able to draw in the net because of the multitude of fish. It was John who said to Peter, "It is the Lord" (Jn. 21:7). With the help of the other disciples, they dragged the net to shore, and there they saw Jesus next to a fire with fish and bread already cooked. Calling them to him he took of the bread and fish and served his disciples (Jn.21.:8-13). How incredible it is that the one who defeated death, conquered the grave, destroyed the works of the devil, who is the King of kings and Lord of lords was willing to serve his disciples breakfast in the early morning hours of that spring day.

This was the third time Jesus met with his disciples after the resurrection (Jn. 21:14). He had not yet had a personal conversation with Peter since that time when Peter swore his allegiance to Jesus at any cost, saying, "Though all men shall be offended because of you, yet I will never be offended," (Mt. 26:33) and later announcing, "Even if I have to die with You, I will not deny you" (Mt. 26:35 AMP). These words of Peter were challenged by Jesus at that final Passover meal when Jesus warned Peter of the great temptation that lay ahead of him, saying, "Simon, Simon, behold, Satan has desired to have you…But I have prayed for you, that your faith fail not" (Lk. 22:31). Three times in the garden Jesus tried to get Peter and the others to pray so they would not enter into temptation, but each time Jesus approached them, they were sleeping instead. Although Peter was so bold and boastful before Jesus and the other disciples when they were alone, when he was challenged by the authorities, he denied Jesus three times. Peter cursed and swore that he did not know Jesus, but when the rooster crowed, he remembered the warnings Jesus had given him, and he wept bitterly (Mt. 26:74,75).

Peter's guilt and shame must have been overwhelming. Even when the angel spoke to the women at the tomb, he said to them, "Go your way, tell his disciples and Peter" that Jesus is risen (Mk. 16:7). Possibly, Peter no longer considered himself worthy to be Jesus' disciple after denying him three times.

Jesus was not willing to leave Peter in that condition of shame, so after breakfast, Jesus went to Peter and said to him, "Simon, son of Jonas, do you love me more than these? (Jn. 21:15 NKJV). Peter's response was, "Yes, Lord; You know that I love You." Three times Jesus asked Peter the same question, and three times Peter answered the same. It appears that each time the question was asked Peter became more disturbed until he said, "Lord, You know all things; You know that I love you" (Jn. 21:16 NKJV).

What may not be obvious to the casual reader in the English translation is the real question Jesus was asking Peter. The first and second time Jesus asked Peter if he loved him, Jesus used the Greek word *agapao*. This word is translated love, but it is a love that is totally committed and faithful and not based on feelings or circumstances. Peter's answer to Jesus' question the first two times was "Yes, Lord; you know I love you." The Greek word Peter uses in his reply to Jesus is not *agapao*, but *phileo*. *Phileo* carries the meaning of friendship, good feelings, more like a casual acquaintance. Basically, Peter was saying to Jesus something like "Lord, you know that I like you, but obviously I'm not committed to you." Twice Jesus asked Peter the same thing, using the word *agapao* and both times, Peter answered using the word *phileo*. Then, Jesus asked Peter the third time, but this time Jesus used the word *phileo*; that is when Peter became grieved and said, "Lord, you know all things" (Jn. 21:16 NKJV).

What is interesting to me is that, each time Peter responded to Jesus in a way that identified his lack of commitment, Jesus would say to him, "Feed my lambs" or "Feed my sheep." (Jn. 21:15-17). In other words, Jesus was saying to Peter, "I know you are not as committed to me as you thought you were but just keep on doing what I have called you to do." Then Jesus gave Peter some good news, "Most assuredly, I say to you, when you were younger, you girded yourself and walked where you wished; but when you are old, you will stretch out your hands, and another will gird you and carry you where you do not wish" (Jn. 21:18). Jesus' words may sound a little puzzling, but the next verse explains that Jesus was signifying by what death Peter should glorify God.

Jesus was saying to Peter, "You may not be committed to me now to the point that you are willing to lay down your life, but there will come a time when you will choose to stretch out your hands in crucifixion and not deny me." While that may not sound like good news to us, to Peter, it was a prophetic word that, if he would just keep on doing what the Lord had called him to do, his life and death would bring glory to God.

The Great Commission

Jesus was preparing the disciples for his departure and his assignment for them is described in Matthew's gospel. Before he ascended into Heaven he commissioned his followers, saying,

> "All authority has been given to Me in heaven and on earth. Go therefore and make disciples of all nations, baptizing them in the name of the Father and of the Son and of the Holy Spirit, teaching them to observe all things that I have commanded you; and lo, I am with you always, even to the end of the age" (Mt. 28:18-20 NKJV).

They were to go in the authority of the name of Jesus and, not only preach the gospel, but also make disciples of all nations. They were to teach those who believed to observe (guard from loss or injury) everything Jesus had taught them.

This commissioning was obviously not just for the twelve or the seventy, but it was for all believers for all time. In fact, Paul writes in his letter to Timothy, "And the things which you have heard of me among many witnesses, commit thou the same to faithful men, who shall be able to teach others also" (2 Tim. 2:2 ASV).

As believers carried the gospel, they also were to give demonstration of the kingdom of God, as Paul writes to the Corinthians, "For the kingdom of God is not in word, but in power" (1 Cor. 4:20). In his first letter to the Thessalonians Paul declares, "For our gospel came not unto you in word only, but also in power, and in the Holy Spirit…" (1 Thess. 1:5). These scriptures that reference events that happened decades after the resurrection of Jesus demonstrate the success of those original disciples Jesus commissioned years before.

Chapter 19

The Ascension

During the forty days following his resurrection, Jesus appeared to many people but not to everyone. When Peter was preaching to the gentiles at Cornelius' house, he said concerning Jesus, "Him God raised up the third day, and showed him openly; not to all the people, but unto witnesses chosen before of God" (Acts 10:40,41). We know that list of witnesses included Mary of Magdala, Mary the mother of Jesus, his eleven disciples, and his brethren. Then, Paul wrote that more than five hundred at one time saw him (1 Cor. 15:6).

The five hundred or more that saw Jesus were most likely those who were with him on the Mount of Olives when he spoke to them just before he ascended into heaven. Here, we read Luke's description of those forty days when Jesus, "showed himself alive after his passion by many infallible proofs…and speaking of the things pertaining to the kingdom of God" (Acts 1:3). Jesus first instructed all those who had assembled on the Mount of Olives to wait for the promise of the Father, which was the baptism with the Holy Spirit (Acts 1:4,5).

Someone asked Jesus about restoring the kingdom to Israel, but his reply was not to concern themselves about times and seasons but instead wait for the promised Holy Spirit (Acts 1:6-8).

Jesus had spoken at length to his disciples about their need to receive the Holy Spirit. Jesus said it was expedient for them that he should go so that the Holy Spirit would come (Jn. 16:7). As long as Jesus remained in the earth, the Spirit anointed him alone, but when he returned to heaven, he would send the Spirit of God to anoint and empower every believer.

Jesus announced to the crowd on the Mount of Olives that they would receive power to be witnesses of him first in the city of Jerusalem, then in all of Judea, then in the land of Samaria, and from there to the ends of the earth (Acts 1:8). Having said this, Jesus was lifted up into a cloud from the Mount of Olives.

People's first impression when reading these scriptures is usually of Jesus beginning to slowly ascend from the earth until he disappears in the fluffy, white clouds above, but are those the kinds of clouds described here?

There are many references to God coming in clouds. Jesus told the high priest that he would see the Son of man sitting on the right hand of power and coming in the clouds of heaven (Mk. 14:62). This coming is usually in reference to judgment. In the Book of Isaiah, God is described as advancing against Egypt, riding on a swift cloud (Isa. 19:1).

"A cloud of witnesses" is described in the Book of Hebrews (12:1) and seems to refer to the many heroes of faith mentioned in chapter eleven. Psalms describes the "chariots of God" as myriads and myriads of angels (Ps. 68:17) and the next verse mentions that one would ascend "on high" and lead "captivity captive": and receive "gifts for men." (68:18) which is the verse Paul quoted in regards to Jesus (Eph. 4:8). The Book of Daniel describes a vision Daniel had. This prophet proclaims, "I saw in the night visions, and, behold, one like the Son of man came with clouds of heaven, and came to the Ancient of days, and they brought him near before him" (Dan. 7:13). It seems that the 'cloud' is referred to as 'them' who brought the Son of man to God the Father who is called the Ancient of days. With these things in mind we can see that the cloud that Jesus ascended into must have been the cloud of angels and not just some fluffy cloud we might see on a summer day.

Jesus ascended as the five hundred were gazing up into heaven. Suddenly, two men (angels) appeared and addressed the crowd, saying, "Men of Galilee, why do you stand gazing up into heaven? This same Jesus, who was taken up from you into heaven, will so come in like manner as you saw him go into heaven" (Acts 1:11 NKJV). After the angel spoke, the crowd dispersed and returned to the city of Jerusalem just a short walk across the Kidron valley. In an upper room in the city of Jerusalem, the eleven gathered with the women, Mary the mother of Jesus, and his brethren. It would be these who numbered one hundred and twenty who would wait for ten days until the Feast of Pentecost and the coming of the Holy Spirit.

With the baptism in the Holy Spirit and the empowering of the one hundred and twenty, the Church began the mission of taking the gospel of Jesus Christ to the ends of the earth. Now, nearly two thousand years later, we can read in history books of the wonderful works of God throughout the centuries. In every nation there are those who hold the truth of the Lordship of Jesus Christ and carry the love of God. This mission will continue until, "…the earth shall be full of the knowledge of the LORD, as the waters cover the sea" (Isa. 11:9).

A daily devotional designed to gather together a busy family before each member hurries off to begin their day. Each days' devotional features a scripture, a promise or command, prayer, proclamation, memory verse, blessing, and hugs.

$12.00
(When Purchased through Coflin Family Publishing):
DAN@COFLIN.COM

Also available through:
Amazon.com

"Dr. Dan's "Faith Family Minute" is a great tool for Dads and Moms to lead their families in daily devotion to Christ. It builds faith and a culture of caring. I highly recommend its reading and application to keep Christ at the center of your home."
-Dr. Daniel Bernard

www.ingramcontent.com/pod-product-compliance
Lightning Source LLC
Chambersburg PA
CBHW070543010526
44118CB00012B/1206